From Shadows of Darkness to Silhouettes of Hope

From Shadows of Darkness to Silhouettes of Hope

By

Dorothy Henderson Boozer

Strategic Book Publishing and Rights Co.

Copyright © 2013 Dorothy Henderson Boozer. All rights reserved.

No part of this book may be reproduced or transmitted in any form or by any means, graphic, electronic, or mechanical, including photocopying, recording, taping, or by any information storage retrieval system, without the permission, in writing, of the publisher.

Strategic Book Publishing and Rights Co.
12620 FM 1960, Suite A4-507
Houston TX 77065
www.sbpra.com

ISBN: 978-1-62516-072-0

DEDICATION

Dedicated to my loving family whose support throughout my life has enabled me to pursue this important mission.

ACKNOWLEDGMENTS

I would like to thank my family for supporting my decisions throughout the years that led me through an incredible journey; one of exploration and desire to fulfill a curiosity, which eventually led to a discovery of truths that brought about an awareness of a great need for transformation within myself and a subsequent reformation within some of the religious orders of the Roman Catholic Church in the USA.

I would also like to thank my spiritual director, a priest, who believed in my journey and put all his trust in God throughout the years that tested my faith beyond belief.

To the Roman Catholic Church, I offer deep gratitude for the three-year investigation of women religious orders in the United States of America, which did confirm truths uncovered throughout my own, personal journey.

My greatest gratitude is offered to my Lord. It was only through His strength, His grace, and His guidance that I endured this journey of great suffering.

My suffering and frustration were not very graceful at times, and for that I apologize. As you enter into this book, you will learn of only a fraction of the suffering I endured throughout my years of searching. There is no possible way to capture the depth of pain, the depth of betrayal, or the loss of trust encountered throughout this journey that eventually led me to the greatest peace, the greatest joy, and a passion to reform that which had gone astray. I am grateful to those who stood by me throughout this great suffering and for those who will continue to stand by me in the coming years as I continue to bring about an awareness of a great need for a vocation ministry for men and women within the Catholic Church. I see a need for a ministry to serve and protect those men and women who seek to serve God by serving His church within a religious order recognized by the Roman Catholic Church.

I have no doubt in my mind that God's hand was in this journey, leading me every step of the way. Therefore, a portion of profits received from this story will be used to establish a vocation ministry for men and women or a discernment ministry for all ages.

A special thanks to my editor.

Edited by Bette Reed, mereed53@hotmail.com

TABLE OF CONTENTS

Part I: Early Formation of Faith..1
Chapter 1: The Seed..3
Chapter 2: The Drought 9
Chapter 3: The Missing Sacrament..15
Chapter 4: Coming Home 20
Chapter 5: Revelations of Hope...24

Part II: Total Commitment to God 29
Chapter 6: Holy/Hell..31
Chapter 7: Come Follow Me..34
Chapter 8: Come and See...39
Chapter 9: Acceptance 51
Chapter 10: Proceed with Caution 60

Part III: Obedience to God...65
Chapter 11: The Flight 67
Chapter 12: Entrance..73
Chapter 13: Suggestive Thinking...78
Chapter 14: Pushing the Breaking Point......................................87
Chapter 15: Outside Influence 92

Part IV: Breaking Away 103
Chapter 16: The Decision 105
Chapter 17: The Escape 115
Chapter 18: The Flight Home 123
Conclusion: The Mission 129

PART I

EARLY FORMATION OF FAITH

CHAPTER 1

THE SEED

As a child, I remember watching *The Flying Nun,* a popular television show in the 60's. I very much admired this nun and secretly wanted to be her when I grew up. It wasn't the flying that interested me so much; it was the people whom she helped that caught my interest. Don't get me wrong, the flying part would have been a cool bonus, and I would never have objected to soaring right into a situation in need of my service. It was one of those rare shows that offered a little fantasy that captured one's interest.

At the age of eight, I had a desire to uncover the mysterious lives of these women who were clothed in very unattractive dresses, living in a world in which they did not fit. I had no desire for the clothing whatsoever, especially those sheets draped over their heads and under their chins, which seemed to squeeze their cheeks right over the corners of their mouths, creating a resemblance of a wooden puppet. *Why did they wear them anyway?* They seemed to be more of a hassle than a benefit, but what did I know? I was only a kid. I had so many unanswered questions about these unique women who were beneath layers and layers of clothing. *Where did they live? What did they do when they weren't helping people? Why don't they talk to us kids like they did on television?*

I didn't have the opportunity to ask them any of these questions as I, like most other children in the neighborhood, attended public school, and they were only allowed to teach at Catholic schools. In fact, I was only around them for a brief time once a week for religious education. There was just not enough time to become acquainted or even have a conversation with them. Our weekly classes began by gathering on the playground until the bell rang, at which time we formed lines in total silence. *How could I get to know them better when we were silenced at the sound of the bell?* They didn't mingle with the kids on the playground. In fact, they kept their distance from us until the bell rang.

We did not speak in class unless we were called upon, which was the norm for all classroom education back then...at least in the northern part of the country. You dared not raise your hand to ask a question that didn't pertain to the classroom material being presented. Therefore, the opportunity to explore the possibility of a life of service was not even an option for me. The fear of being ridiculed prevented me from speaking in class. Being ridiculed in front of my classmates was something I tried to avoid, quickly molding me into silence.

Who even knew where nuns came from anyway? It wasn't a topic that was ever discussed. Maybe they were just born into the church! Maybe they had to be extra holy and enter by invitation only. Nobody seemed to talk about it.

They just appeared, just like babies appeared. The stork delivered babies, so maybe angels delivered the nuns to places they needed to be. *Who knew?* Maybe only God knew, and their lives would always remain a mystery to me.

I was fortunate to live in a very safe neighborhood where the school, the main street, and even the church were all within walking distance. I remember walking down to the church with a friend one day, during a time when mass wasn't being celebrated. She had no interest in exploring the church and ran on ahead to a nearby store to purchase an Italian Ice, leaving me alone to explore that which made me so curious.

I quickly ran up the stairs, peering over my shoulders to be sure nobody saw me sneaking up to the door. Much to my surprise, the door was open! *Who knew the doors of the church were open even when mass wasn't being celebrated?* I wondered if they even knew they had left the door unlocked. I immediately knew I would not tell anyone, because I wanted to come back for more secret visits. Although I had a slight fear of being caught, I had a much greater curiosity to discover what was behind the large wooden door when the church was unoccupied.

As I opened the door, a beam of sunlight slowly peeked through the crack, giving light to the darkness. I remember the smell of burning candles and the lingering scent of "church." It was so dark and totally empty.

My eyes wandered around the church until I found the little room, or box as I often referred to it, made especially for the Sacrament of Reconciliation. I wanted to know more about that little box since I would soon be making my first confession. The whole thing was pretty scary. No kid wants to enter a dark room by themselves in the first place. The thought of entering a small room and pulling a curtain behind me consumed my thoughts. My stomach seemed to be turning flips. I wanted to get a closer look, but fear consumed me. I would surely get caught or, even worse, somebody might jump out from behind the curtain. *What if the church door locked behind me?* Nobody would ever know where I was. I could actually be here until next weekend when the "church people" came back. I would surely be in a heap of trouble then. It would always be a mystery as to what really went on in an empty church, or so I thought.

I guess I was too young to realize other people must have entered the church to light candles, which were flickering in the darkness. I guess I was too young to know the church then was actually open twenty-four hours a day, seven days a week, for anyone to come in and spend time with God in prayer. I guess I was too young to understand the desire that was beginning to develop from within myself.

We went to church every Sunday, but there was something different about being in that same church when it was full of people. I was too short to even see what was going on up there on the "the stage," otherwise known as the altar. That desire to be in the church when I passed by during the day seemed to diminish when the church was full of people. I would sit in my pew, staring at the backs of tall people, except when my Dad let me sit on the end of the pew. On those days, I could at least stretch my head around their backs while I stood on the kneeler, gripping the side of the pew. As I swung out into the aisle, I got very quick glances, before I was reeled back in with a firm grip of my Father's hand, right between my shoulder and elbow. It was a useless attempt to see the altar. My view consisted of rear ends until I grew a little taller. In the meantime, I just couldn't wait to go home. I estimated the time of escape by the bells ringing about midway through the mass. That was my cue...we were half-way finished.

Oh, if I only knew at that time what those bells truly meant! I was too young to know, too young to understand. One day, I would recognize the true value of those bells. One day, I would come to the realization that at the sound of the bells, the gifts laid upon the altar were being transformed into the true Body and Blood of Christ and, within a few minutes, He would be offered to those who walked down the aisle to receive Him. Those same bells, which were once used to determine how much longer I had to sit, would eventually be recognized as the sound of God's presence among us. I was too young to know, too young to understand this precious gift.

Finally, the day came to celebrate my First Confession, and I was so excited about it. This meant that I, too, would soon be offered Communion and maybe, just maybe, I would understand a little more about what was really going on in church.

Our Reconciliation class was seated up front in the church. I was excited, because I could actually see everything. On this day, however, there was nothing to see. It was very quiet and dimly lit. We were sitting in lines going over the prayers we would soon recite in the darkness of the dreaded box. I wasn't afraid of

From Shadows of Darkness to Silhouettes of Hope

the sacrament. I was afraid of the box. I didn't know what was going to happen when I entered into the darkness and pulled the curtain behind me. Yes, I knew the prayers, but nobody can prepare a child for this dreadful, mysterious, dark box.

As I entered, I couldn't see until my eyes adjusted to the light or, rather, the lack of light. I can remember the damp, musty smell, which reminded me of an old basement. I couldn't wait to get out. I slowly found the place to kneel, while trying not to touch anything, and began my confession. It was so dark, and I really couldn't see. Therefore, I figured if the priest couldn't see me very well, he probably couldn't hear me very well either. I wanted him to hear me, because I wanted all my sins to be forgiven. Our teachers had never really explained what sin was, other than "as children you either lie or steal." Those were the examples given to us in religious education classes. *Hmmmmm, I guess maybe I've taken something from my sister without asking for it...so yes, I guess that's stealing.* Hmmmmm, if we don't tell the truth, we'd surely get into lots of trouble when it was discovered. Maybe I had lied and just didn't remember it, because we're all sinners. *What if I had forgotten something, and I didn't confess it?* Maybe I better cover all my bases. *Yes! That's it!* We had to go to confession once a week, and you had to confess something every week. I know...I could confess in advance. That way, if I did not tell the truth for some reason during the week, I'd be covered. I took a deep breath and proudly began to tell the priest my sins. I wanted to be sure he heard them, because I surely didn't want to repeat them! BLESS ME FATHER FOR I HAVE SINNED...

The priest had no trouble hearing my confession. Neither did the whole class! But hey, I was covered, because I even confessed to lying and stealing things that never even took place. Every week, I went to confession and proudly confessed things I didn't do...just in case, to make up for anything I didn't remember or might do in the future. They were the only two sins I really knew: not telling the truth and taking things without permission.

I'm sure if the priest ever recognized me on the street, he would greet me with a smile outside, but inside I'm sure he would be whispering to himself, "Here comes that lying little thief."

I felt sure the other kids were doing the same thing. One of my friends took something from the grocery store, and her mother made her return it. I went with her for moral support, adding a little advice on the way home to make her feel better about her sin. "Hey, look on the bright side! Now you have something you can REALLY confess."

I didn't truly grasp the idea of confession at this age, and neither did my friends. I honestly don't know if it was the way it was taught or the way it was received. It was something we had to do in order to receive communion. Therefore, we participated to the best of our ability, which obviously wasn't very good.

Soon after, I received my First Communion, which went much smoother than my first confession. On that day I knew there was more, something nobody seemed to grasp or even had been able to teach. *Could anyone ever really teach such an incredible gift as the Eucharist in such a fashion that would be totally understood by everyone?* It was beyond our understanding, and I secretly thought my teachers didn't even understand it enough themselves.

We gathered for a class picture on those same stairs that led up to the mysterious church door. Those same stairs were the ones I climbed so frequently in search of something of which I was not yet aware. I knew this mystery would continue, and one day I would be able to understand the depth of this desire that seemed to consume me. I knew without a shadow of a doubt that there was something more. There was something so special here that I just didn't quite grasp yet.

CHAPTER 2

THE DROUGHT

As time went by, at the age of ten, our family transferred to Alabama due to my father's job. We never lived within walking distance of a Catholic church again. That curiosity and desire to know more about this wonderful faith seemed to have been pushed aside when we moved to this new place called Alabama. I was beginning to wonder if it was even on the same planet as Connecticut, the place with the mysterious church, where everyone was Catholic.

Were there even any Catholics who lived in Alabama? Could we be the only Catholics in this bizarre place? I now felt as if I was an alien and had landed on another planet. I was now in a place known as "The Bible Belt" surrounded by Protestants who made faces when I proudly announced I was Catholic. Kids can be cruel. I now was ridiculed for the mysterious faith I had such a desire to understand. I longed to find an empty church where I could be alone. I still wanted to know and understand this desire to be in an empty church.

It was not quite as bad as I thought. Once religious education classes, Catechism of Catholic Doctrine (CCD) started, I realized I wasn't the only Catholic in my school. There was actually one more! Neither of us talked about it very much, only when we were alone. Even then, it was only to ask if we went to church on Sunday. That's when I realized how "freakish" kids thought this Catholic religion really was. One day, on the playground, I proudly announced that I went to mass on Saturday, not realizing I was being overheard by another student. That was the moment, that very moment, when I was really made to feel like I didn't belong in this strange place called Alabama!

"What are you?" the kid asked. "Don't you even believe in Jesus?" he continued. "Sunday is the day of worship, everyone knows that!" he announced as he walked away in disgust.

It was on that day, I pretty much decided if I wanted any friends, I would have to keep my faith to myself.

I actually did make a lot of friends, once I stopped talking about my faith. At the age of ten, friends were really important. This is where we lived now, and I had to get used to it.

I always liked moving, and I always adjusted just fine. Although, this was the first time I had ever encountered a problem in a new school. My parents always made sure we had opportunities to make friends in our new homes and quickly planned a sleepover for the people we had met in the neighborhood. It was great, and I knew we were going to be just fine...as long as we never told anyone we were Catholic.

Kids forget quickly, and life in Alabama was beginning to be fun. Of course, there were many other adjustments to the South, such as food, discipline, and accents to name a few. But none of these compared to the biggest challenge of our faith.

God works in mysterious ways. If I had remained up north, who knows? I may have always just gone through the motions and never had the opportunity to really grasp the meaning and depth of my faith.

Where were we anyway? I knew nothing about Alabama or life in the South other than the story of Huck Finn. All I knew at the age of ten was that I would go to school in cut-off jeans and bare feet, just like in the movies. I was really excited about cut-offs, since we had to wear dresses to school every day, up in the "real world." Much to my surprise, I did have to wear shoes to school and cut-off shorts were worn only at home. Bummer.

From Shadows of Darkness to Silhouettes of Hope

Another disappointment. The one thing I was looking forward to was not going to become a reality.

This adventure was becoming a nightmare. The next big challenge was enduring the language barrier. When people opened their mouths to speak, I couldn't understand a word they were saying. "I thought these folks spoke English!" The words came out about as fast as they crossed the street! *Why did people speak and move so slowly in the South?* I remember the first time we had to wait for people to cross the street before we could make a right-hand turn when the light was red. That is completely another story. Ten cars could have turned before they finally got out of our way. And red means STOP where I come from...not stop and go if you think you can make it! We just laughed and knew we had another story to tell Dad at the dinner table. My family was having the same trouble as I was. Therefore, I did have some company in this boat that appeared to be drifting away from shore. At least we all had something to talk about at the dinner table, and laughter seemed to be the only way to deal with our time of adjustment. My three-year old brother, on the other hand, would be brought up in this land of another world and never be able to shake the accent or the culture. He was going to be a Southerner for life. Bless his little heart!

School continued to be a problem and spelling was most difficult for me. I spelled the words as they were pronounced. As always, it was my fault for my first big fat "F," according to the teacher anyway. I tried to explain how I spelled the words, just like they were pronounced. That did not sit well with her at all. She said if I studied my word list, I would know the words and be able to spell them correctly. Great, now I had to study spelling lists. End result, I failed spelling even with studying. To this day, I still believe I spelled the words correctly. You do not pronounce oil as "all." If you say ALL, I will spell ALL. It was now a matter of principle. Forgetting my place as the student, my goal was to teach my teacher how to speak English correctly. It was a very long year!

Discipline, well, now that took the cake! I was in a foreign place and had to ask many questions. Everyone talked freely and classroom behavior in this place called Alabama was shocking at first, but I soon came to enjoy its entertainment. At least I felt free to ask questions. It seemed, however, if you asked the wrong question, you were being a class clown. If you tried to be a class clown, you got chased with a thick piece of board, in the shape of a paddle, by a very upset lady they called "teacher." Being a terrified ten-year old who had never even been spanked, my instinct was to RUN! Probably not the best decision. Fear of a teacher was something I had never experienced before. *Was it even legal to hit children with a 6" x 12" paddle in this foreign land? Where the heck was I anyway?* I wanted to go home! Back to Connecticut and back to my church. But first things first, I had to get away from this lady who was chasing me with a paddle! I was small, and she was not. My only option was to dodge her by crawling under the desks. The kids, of course, were on my side and moved their legs as I dashed under their seats. When the teacher realized it was hopeless, she stopped and gave me a dreadful look. There was dead silence as she awaited a response from me. I had so much to learn in this new place, and the first thing was how to respond properly to someone chasing you with a paddle. "You're not going to hit me. I'm telling my mother." That was the first thing that popped out of my mouth! Evidently, this wasn't the proper response.

So, this was the introduction to my education in Alabama. I knew it wasn't right to hit children with big fat paddles. The challenge was teaching this to the ones holding the paddles. Her response, "Young lady, you have a lot to learn in this school," and I responded, "You can't hit children with boards where I come from!" Thank God I left off the part about "You have a lot to learn, too!" I guess I was learning very slowly. She never hit me, so I'm guessing maybe she was beginning to understand

From Shadows of Darkness to Silhouettes of Hope

where I was coming from, or maybe she was just tired of dealing with me. Either way, I was content. I never did understand what I said that upset her so, and I dared not ask at that point.

I got home to find my Mother supported me. She stated that if any teacher ever raised her hand or a board to me...Well, just come home! Ha! For a short time, I had support. Dad quickly stepped in and informed us of "education in the South." How could an area known for Southern Hospitality allow someone to hit kids? It didn't make a whole lot of sense to me. Suddenly, I felt as if I were in the Land of Oz. "Toto, I don't think we're in Kansas anymore."

Everything was different here. Even the earth looked different. I wasn't quite sure we were even on the planet Earth anymore. The ground everywhere I had ever been was rich and dark, not a sticky red! The red clay actually looked thirsty; it was so dry. So dry, it even had cracks in it. That's how I felt, as if I were in a desert, thirsting for something other than water, thirsting for something more.

The Catholic church here seemed to be lacking that mysterious quality that stirred my curiosity in Connecticut. It seemed to be as dry as the ground it was built on and just couldn't quench my thirst, even at this young age. I was thirsty but didn't even know what I was thirsting for. All my friends were having so much fun at their churches, and I didn't understand why our classes were so dull and boring. I wanted to go to church where people were happy and had fun with their friends.

We continued going to church, my sister and I, because we were approaching our Confirmation. After that, we could make our own decisions about church.

The only thing I remember about my Confirmation was the slap on the cheek, which I never knew the meaning of, and which is no longer done today. In my little mind, it was a wake-up call. I'm going to die here. I'm going to find a place where church can be fun, a place where people are happy about being at church. I was going to walk away from this dried-up, cracked

13

ground; this desert of a place. I was going to jump into an oasis with my friends who loved their churches. Even as a teenager, I could sense the happiness and joy present in their churches, and I wanted to be a part of it. Yes, I was going to explore Protestantism in the Bible Belt of the South!

CHAPTER 3

THE MISSING SACRAMENT

I was now exploring different churches with friends from school, and I loved it. Finally, I wanted to be in church again.

"Are you saved?" This was the question presented to us over and over again. Not really understanding the question, I remained silent. After all, the question was being presented to us as a class, and nobody was being called on to answer specifically. I immediately had flashbacks of being chased with a paddle for asking a question in elementary school. Therefore, I definitely steered clear of asking questions. I had friends now, and I didn't want to do anything to lose them.

I also avoided any discussions of faith as they, too, seemed to repel friends in a hurry. I dared not talk about this alien faith of Protestantism with my parents either. They were not too happy with my choice to leave the Catholic church. Although my Mom and Dad weren't active in church any longer, Dad was still Catholic at heart and changing religions was a topic to avoid. It wasn't quite as hard for my Mom, since she had been Presbyterian. I do believe they were happy I was associating with a "good" group of friends who went to church. My parents were also happy that we were always doing "church" things rather than hanging out with the wrong crowd. Don't get me wrong, we did have our share of mischief now and then...

So, I found myself alone again in a faith I didn't fully understand. I still had an unsolved problem. *Was I saved?* I studied, researched, and listened very closely. Then the day came, when we were individually asked, the dreaded question, "Are you saved?" *How can you know the answer to a question when you really don't understand the question being asked?*

We were all asked to put our heads down on the desk and close our eyes. The big question was asked again. "Are you saved?" A terrifying feeling came over me, and I could feel myself tremble. I had not finished my research on this project, and I had no idea if I was saved! We were asked to raise our hand if we had been saved. *Saved from what? Saved from whom?* I knew I must raise my hand if I were saved! That image came through my head again of the teacher chasing me with a paddle. *Was I going to get hit if I'm not saved?* Well, I was not going to go through that again. I raised my hand as I contemplated the seven sacraments. It seemed like an hour. I don't know what she was doing all that time...maybe making a list of everyone who was not saved? *Who knew?* Maybe they would be asked to leave the church if they weren't saved. I'm thankful my hand was up, at least half-way. I thought half-way was a good choice for someone who didn't know the answer to a really complicated question. I was thinking that if she couldn't explain the question so we could understand it, she probably shouldn't be teaching it. *Who knew?* Maybe I was saved. Maybe being saved is actually in one of those sacraments that I was quietly contemplating. I remembered the Catholic teachers couldn't really teach the Eucharist. Therefore, maybe this was also a mystery that was just too difficult to teach.

A terrifying feeling rushed through my body as I realized the Catholic church must have left out a very important sacrament of being saved, because the only way you can get to heaven is if you're saved! Great. I was then consumed with a terrifying fear and felt my body quickly heat up. Little beads of perspiration began to form on my forehead. Finally, we were allowed to open our eyes, and Sunday school was over. What a relief. I couldn't get out of that room fast enough! The teacher's final words, "Remember, the altar call is at the end of church. If you want to accept Jesus as your personal savior, be saved, and be promised a place in heaven, come to the altar and accept him today."

Okay. I was thinking I would do this. I wanted to go to heaven. But, I still didn't understand what I was supposed to do when I got to the altar. It was not clear. *What would they do to me? Was I going to get slapped one more time, like when I was confirmed?* As we entered the church, I was confident that I would survive whatever was going to happen. I wanted to get to heaven. My thoughts quickly turned to the Catholic church, and I wondered how they could have left out such an important sacrament.

As I sat through the service, my mind began to wander. I raised my hand to say that I was already saved. *Can a person be saved twice?* No, they will think I am a liar. Back to being a liar again. *Would I even be allowed back into the Catholic church to go to confession? Am I still Catholic?* Once again, I was an alien in a foreign land, and I did not understand. I wanted to go back to Connecticut where everyone was Catholic, and if they weren't, they didn't go around asking everyone if they were "saved"! *Why was everything so complicated here in the South?* My thoughts continued, "My only way to get to heaven is to be saved, but it will have to be at a church where they didn't think I was already saved."

I really needed to notify the Catholic church and let them know about this being saved thing. All these Catholics are celebrating the seven sacraments, and the most important one is missing...the one that will get them into heaven!

The whole event was so traumatic that I never went back to this Protestant church. Soon after, some other friends invited me to their church. I got involved in the youth group and looked forward to church every Sunday morning and evening and on Wednesday nights. I loved it! They didn't make you raise your hand with your eyes closed, and I felt so comfortable there.

I loved this church so much. All the kids met at church, and we all sat together. The adults spoke to us and welcomed all of us! We all were accepted. They had the same altar call, but it wasn't so traumatic. I wanted to go to heaven, and I knew if I didn't walk down that aisle I wouldn't get there. So, one Sunday night, I walked the aisle. Not really knowing what to do or say, I watched as others felt the call from the Holy Spirit. The preacher reached out to them, welcoming them into God's church. There was great joy. When he got to me, I thought I should tell him where I came from, because I had heard comments against Catholics from some of their congregation. I feared what would happen once they found out. I hesitated and quietly said, "I'm Catholic." His response was not as condemning as the others. In fact, it was with a sympathetic voice that he responded, "That's okay. We accept anyone, and you will be baptized soon." I was excited to tell him about my baptism as a Catholic, but he said they didn't acknowledge infant baptisms, and I would have to be baptized again. My heart broke, as if an arrow had pierced right through it. I was being rejected for who I was and for the age when I was baptized...and right there in front of the entire church at the altar! I was just a teenager, but even I noticed the difference in his facial expression and his welcoming, which was more sympathetic, because I was Catholic. I quickly turned my thoughts to heaven. This was only a small suffering, and I could endure it. I was now going to be welcomed in heaven.

Yes, now my bases were covered at both the Catholic church and the Baptist church! I really didn't know whom to believe at that time, so I would do whatever they said just to get to heaven where I would have that mysterious feeling that I continued to seek. I had received all my sacraments at the Catholic church, I was now saved, and I would soon be baptized again. All my bases would soon be covered. It was my greatest desire to find the truth and to know I would be in heaven for eternity.

As time went by, I really began to understand more about the different denominations and how they all believe different things. There were just too many denominations all claiming to hold the truth. This can be pretty traumatic to a young person, especially when your true faith of Catholicism was being put down by other denominations. After all, I was still Catholic at heart. I just wanted to go to heaven.

CHAPTER 4

COMING HOME

I was now in my mid twenties, married, and had a child, Christopher. It was my desire to raise Christopher in church, and I longed to find the right one. I tried a "non-denominational" church, but it was not for me. Most of my time was spent in the parking lot throwing stones, because Chris had no interest in sitting still for an hour. Much to my surprise, it was a great time for contemplation. My heart was yearning for something, but I just couldn't find it.

Frustrated with all religions and the search for "home," I resorted to no church at all. At least there was not that conflict of the heart being pulled in different directions anymore. There was no longer the trauma of finding "the right denomination" in search of the truth anymore. I now had a true view of religion and denominations. I really wasn't sure any of them were right. *Did anyone really even know what the truth was any more? Did anyone really even see what was going on with all these different denominations, each claiming to hold the truth?*

No wonder there was such a high percentage of people declaring to be Christians who didn't attend church. There was emptiness, a longing for that mysterious feeling I had had in second grade that was lost forever...so I thought. *Did anyone really know where the truth lies?*

Several years later, at the age of twenty-eight, and married for the second time...everything changed. It all took place very quickly while preparing dinner for a friend, who was expected to arrive at any time. I always looked forward to her visits and was very excited for the chance to see her again. As the afternoon progressed, an unexplainable event took place. This event took me by surprise, and I did not know what was happening. It was so powerful, so strong, that I did exactly what was asked of me. There was no other option.

I heard the words "Come to the church." It was so clear, no misunderstanding. I dared not ignore it. My mind was racing. *What?* I was cooking dinner for company. I had Christopher to care for. *How could I do this? Which church?* My mind quickly took me back in time to the church in Connecticut. I was not even attending a church at the time! The religious turmoil was over, the trauma was gone. I don't want this to start all over again. It's Saturday. It was not even a church day. There was no time to figure this all out. I had to do it. I had to do it now.

My husband of about a year walked through the door. I greeted him quickly and stated that I had to go to church. He was baffled and reminded me that we had company coming for dinner.

It was my best friend. She would understand. I confidently stated, "Just give her a beer, and I'll finish dinner as soon as I get back." He was appalled at my behavior and insisted on knowing where I was going. I responded, "Church, I must go to church." He quickly reminded me that I didn't go to church and wondered what church I was going to! He was not happy, but there was no stopping me. He was more concerned about how to entertain our guest and, more importantly, how to explain my bizarre behavior to her.

As I ran to the car, I began to ask God where He was taking me, because I had no idea where I was going.

I drove straight to the Catholic church. The feeling was too strong to say no. I did not know a soul in that church and did not know why I was being drawn to it. It wasn't time for mass after all; it was Saturday afternoon.

I quickly remembered the mysterious feeling of the church in Connecticut, as I walked toward the door. I was afraid in a way, but this time I was older. I had hoped the door would open, just like the one in Connecticut. There was a difference though, I was on the main street, right in the middle of town, and didn't care who saw me. I didn't have to hide. The mysterious feeling peaked as I tried to open the door. Much to my surprise, it was open! The church was beautiful...not like I had remembered it from thirteen years ago. The church was so peaceful that it took my breath away! I had no fear as I walked down the aisle. I could smell the "church smell" and see the candles flickering in the dimly-lit building. I looked around. Nobody was there, and I was alone with the mysterious church feeling all to myself. Out of the corner of my eye, I saw the box, the confessional room. I was so drawn to it and walked in as if I knew what I was doing. Much to my surprise, there was a priest in there. I must have looked dazed, because I was startled, and I had just experienced something of the unexplainable. I couldn't speak. The only words I remembered were, "I don't know why I'm here...I want to come home."

I couldn't tell the truth of what had just happened. The priest probably wouldn't believe me anyway. The most important thing was that I was home, and God's words are what brought me there. I listened, and He brought me home.

I couldn't control my tears. I wanted to confess my sins, but how can you confess thirteen years of sins? I did not even remember how the Confession was supposed to go. I just remember the priest's welcome. It was a warm welcome, and I knew this is where I belonged. Of course, I stayed in the empty church for a little while longer. I didn't want to leave.

I remember telling God, "I looked everywhere for you, but I couldn't find you." He responded "My child, I found you. Go and teach what you have discovered."

I knew my suffering was not only for me. I knew I must teach what I had stumbled upon. It was important to God, and therefore, it was important to me.

I began my studies and went to some Rite of Christian Initiation for Adults (RCIA) classes to refresh myself. After much studying, I realized that yes, we are saved. We just didn't use those exact words in teaching the sacraments.

The Catholic church had not left out a sacrament. I was then determined to teach Catholic children the truth. I did not want any of them to go through what I went through. It is difficult being Catholic in the Bible Belt. Catholics must know their faith and be confident in teaching it. More importantly, they must share it.

We not only have the seven sacraments to share in God's grace, we live our Catholic faith every day of our lives. Our faith determines our decisions. What a treasure I had found! Yes, He would turn this desert into an oasis.

I was so thankful for my desert and so grateful for God's spoken word to me on that day when He truly brought me back home! Not only am I saved, I have been given a gift; a gift of faith. Now, I accept Jesus, my savior, every time I walk down the aisle to receive Him in the Eucharist!

I give thanks to my Lord who guides me when I wander off the path, for His gentle hand returns me to Himself...for that which was destined for me all along.

Yes, He has turned my shadows of darkness into silhouettes of hope! My journey would continue with a new breath of hope. I would share what I had discovered with extreme excitement... just as He commanded!

CHAPTER 5

REVELATIONS OF HOPE

I immediately took my son, Chris, to Mass as I wanted to share what I had discovered with him. I wanted him to celebrate his First Reconciliation and receive his First Communion just as I had. It was difficult entering back into the Catholic church. I was facing unexpected challenges, but was determined to conquer them.

I spent my first year pretty much to myself. It was difficult to enter into the family circle here. It was very different from the Protestant churches where the people reached out and welcomed every new face with a warm smile and eagerly involved them in ministry.

An entire year passed before anyone even spoke to me. *How could I pass on what God had entrusted me with if nobody gave me a chance to speak?* This was going to be more difficult than I had ever expected. It was I who had to reach out to them, which was a reminder of why I had drifted away in the first place. I knew I was where God wanted me to be, and I wasn't going to drift again.

I decided to be proactive. I signed up to volunteer. I enrolled Chris in Catholic School, since he was not interested in Catechism of Catholic Doctrine (CCD) classes. I volunteered for everything I could possibly handle, tightly squeezing and using every minute of my schedule. Eventually I began teaching CCD. It was so much work, more than I ever expected. I finally felt as if I were truly a member of the Catholic Church. I loved who I was becoming, and I loved teaching the faith!

I couldn't teach without studying on my own. I put a tremendous amount of time into teaching a one-hour class once a week. As I taught, I also learned. I kept my Catechism and Bible on my coffee table, referring to them throughout every day. This is our faith, and the Catechism explains what we believe and why we believe it. Every belief is reinforced by scripture, which is referred to on every page. I spent every day for years diving into these Books, which were coming alive right before my eyes.

Finally, I was given the chance to teach a First Communion class. There was no greater gift than preparing others to receive Christ. My own personal experiences were to be used as I taught. God had allowed these sufferings for a reason, and I truly felt they could be beneficial to others. When others benefited from my suffering, it seemed to add meaning and purpose to my life. I wanted to use my experiences to prevent anyone else from going through the same agony that I had endured.

A First Reconciliation retreat was developed to reduce the fear from the dreaded confessional box. It gave the children an opportunity to really understand what confession is. It gave them an opportunity to review and understand what sin is. It also gave them a chance to enter into the confessional room and actually practice what was going to occur. This would lessen any fears they had and focus on the forgiveness and mercy of our Lord in the Sacrament of Reconciliation. It was a "chapel" command, much like the first command, "Come to the church," which I was quickly learning to obey.

As I saw the sufferings of my journey being put into place for others, I began to see my life in a different light. I began to really understand how I could use my life and my experiences for God.

As my journey continued, I realized there was still so much more. God only reveals small portions at a time. He knows we are unable to absorb it all at once. I loved where this journey was leading me. My life had changed so much, and I wanted this transformation to continue. I wanted to keep growing, to spend more time in silence, grasping for more and more.

As my journey continued and the years passed, my husband followed the faith by enrolling in RCIA. My Mom followed, and a few years later, my Dad came back home to the church. I watched God's work as He gently brought so many people home simply because they shared what they had found. Yes, we are truly vessels that God works through. Do not doubt it for a moment. My brother and his wife joined the faith, along with their children. Yes, it was contagious.

I soon found my greatest joy would be welcoming others into the mysterious faith where I found such peace and joy. I loved my life. I loved where I was going and who I was becoming! Circumstances in life did not change, but the way I viewed them certainly took on a new meaning.

Faith changes people. I couldn't go back. I don't think I even knew how to go back if I had wanted to do so. I am no longer who I used to be, but I did know that no matter where this journey took me, I would never be alone. God was with me, and we would walk this path of life together.

Once again, I endured the suffering of a deep loss. God must come first, and what is best for my son must be considered in all circumstances. Another life change would soon take place. I found myself single once again. The change was hard for all involved. One of the hardest decisions was placed before me. Sometimes, when you love someone so much, you must let them go. Place them in God's hands, and trust beyond all understanding.

This is what I had to do for my son. Although it was the hardest thing I have ever been faced with, I had to let my son go, let him make his own decisions. Being a teenager, he wanted to return to his old school, which meant he would have to live with his father. If I didn't allow him to make this decision on his own, our relationship would come to an end. Trusting in his decision and, more importantly, putting my trust in God, I realize today this was the right choice; the only choice. Life is full of choices. Our choices affect others. Sometimes in a good way, sometimes in a bad way. No matter what our choices, no matter what our consequences, God is right there in the midst of it all. He will see us through any circumstance, any loss, and draw us ever so close to Himself in the process, if we allow Him to do so. He gives us space, allowing us to make mistakes and, in the process, draws us in, bringing us to the place He wants us to be.

I can truly say those people I have met with the deepest relationship with God are ones who had to cling to God with all their might...those who have experienced great losses and those who have endured great suffering. It is our choice to cling to God during difficult times and to allow Him to heal us, or we can try to heal ourselves, on our own. Only God can truly transform those shadows of darkness into silhouettes of hope.

PART II

TOTAL COMMITMENT TO GOD

CHAPTER 6

HOLY/HELL

My uncertain journey continued, and I soon found myself with a great deal of time on my hands. Chris had joined the Marines and was now an adult seeking his own journey of service, protecting the freedom of a nation that would soon face the unthinkable. An invasion of the United States, otherwise known as 9/11, brought an attack that shook the nation to its core. This was an act of violence that would forever change the world. *How could such evil exist?*

Those who believe in God must not deny the existence of Satan. God exists, and there is evidence of His work in every aspect of life. The more we learn how to pray, the more we begin to develop a sense of not only God's presence in the world, but also the sense of Satan's real presence in the world.

As my relationship deepened with God, my awareness of His presence all around me was overwhelming. He was in nature, from the delicate petals of a rose to the strength of mighty trees. He was in every person, from the infants whose destiny lay before them, to the elderly whose final destination lay before them. He revealed Himself in every animal, from the tiniest ant struggling to survive through team work, to the largest of animals capable of surviving independently. I was consumed with His presence. Life itself took on a different meaning. The gift of life was coming alive and was so precious.

Even during the tragic day of 9/11, God's presence rose above the presence of evil. Days of horror, death, and chaos turned into random acts of love, compassion, and unity. The country was changed forever as God's grace overpowered the destruction wrought by evil.

Yes, God is truly present in the consequences of evil acts. There is a holiness that surfaces during tragedies where Satan is present. There is proof that God is always with us, even in the midst of Satan's evil plans. The world may be oblivious to spiritual wars going on right before our eyes. The attack of 9/11 was a prime example of the depth of these spiritual battles, this Holy/Hell...a battle that Satan did not win.

As one enters into an intense prayer life, one recognizes the mysterious presence of "Good and Evil" within one's own being. Awareness is created within the depths of one's soul by God. We are creatures who are blind and oblivious to our own evil from within. Only God can prune one's life with such a loving hand. He gently removes that which He cannot use and makes room for new growth and new life. He transforms and prunes His creation back into that which He created.

Transformation is a process of letting God's light expose those evils we have within ourselves. It makes room for Him in our lives. This is a process of great pain and suffering. One sits before the Lord in silence, waiting for His light to shine upon the darkness that only He can enter into with you. The awakening of one's being, the awakening of such awareness is crucial to one's transformation. Together, we can look within. An added grace now allows us to see ourselves with the eyes of our souls.

Yes, we are creatures who are truly blind to Satan and his works of evil. We are blind to our egos, our selfishness, our attitudes, and our own desires. God did not create us that way, nor is it His desire for us to remain that way.

The more time spent with God, the greater the depth of awareness. The greater the awareness, the greater the pain. It is a process of pulling in the good and pushing away the evil, closely resembling the power of the ocean's waves. Unable to withstand the pain, one may run away but is quickly drawn right back for more. The pain and suffering are great, but the love and grace are greater. One cannot stay away from this powerful transformation of prayer.

Transformation is a constant battle. When the self is finally devoid of evil and is pure and clean, we have a vessel that God can use. This vessel can slowly fill up again. Our self desires, however, may creep back into our lives. It is God's desire that this vessel remain empty to receive His grace. It is a process of trying to reach perfection...an unattainable goal that one cannot cease trying to attain.

Yes, this battle between good and evil exists in every person. Therefore, we all suffer the consequences produced by these battles. No one is exempt from these battles, which are created within our individual being. In time, touching others, expanding to larger groups, creating a battle of a much larger scale...a battle of Holy/Hell.

CHAPTER 7

COME FOLLOW ME

When Jesus asked the Apostles to follow Him, they dropped everything and followed. Oh, if it were only that simple today!

Today, one must receive spiritual direction, have a minimum of two years of college, be debt-free, give up good jobs, sell vehicles, provide medical insurance, pay for expensive travel, and hope for approval into the order for further discernment to decide if religious life with a particular order will be a good fit. Somewhere in this long list of requirements, the holiness of it all seems to be diminished, if not totally lost.

Little did I know, this journey would change my life forever, taking on a whole new direction and meaning for my life. Yes, I would be led to a closer relationship with God but not through further transformation. I would be pushed to the depths of isolation, clinging to God in desperation as I willingly followed Him into the depths of an unexpected darkness...an unexpected Holy/Hell.

After approximately seven years of spiritual direction and discernment, I was ready to search for an order. Yes, I wanted to continue my journey with God. I wanted to continue this transformation that seemed to consume me. I loved who I was becoming, and I loved the thought of working with the poor. God was holding Chris, who also chose a life of service, in the palm of His hands, and I trusted like never before.

There were obvious barriers that only God could remove. I well remember my prayer of faith: I will go, but there are many barriers that only You can remove. Remove them Lord, and I will follow. As I worked, the barriers fell down, one by one.

As He continued to knock down every barrier standing in my way, I began to feel anxious and in awe at the same time. He was paving the way. The road was clear, and "no" was not an option. *How could I turn back after He had provided the way?* I couldn't bear to hear His words at the end of my life: I paved the way, and you did not follow. I had to follow His way.

As my journey continued, I began to stumble over some unexpected truths. After years of spiritual direction, the first step was to find an order that would be appropriate as my possible destination.

A spiritual director is one who helps you discern how God is working in your life. They do not make decisions for you; they are more of a companion on the journey. They challenge you and help you grow. They keep you grounded and help you in your transformation as your relationship develops with God. The only way to learn about the hundreds, if not thousands, of religious orders is to explore, visit, and get to know them through personal contact. *Where was I to begin?* There were so many orders to explore!

I sought help from the Diocesan Vocation Department, a ministry that supports those discerning the priesthood and/or religious life. My first contact would be to send an e-mail. They would advise me on what to do and how to get started. I waited anxiously for a response. Days passed and finally I got a response. I couldn't wait to accept their advice.

I eagerly opened the e-mail, only to find the heavy words of rejection. "We only serve men seeking a vocation." *What? Why?* I knew the work of the vocation office. They walked every step of the way with the men discerning priesthood. They helped financially throughout their journey as seminarians and made frequent visits to monitor their journey and progress. I was shocked to be rejected by a ministry within the church that was established to help those seeking to serve God by serving the church. *Why wouldn't they serve women?* Both men and women give their lives in service to God. My heart sank from the weight of the words. I was on my own. It was a task proven to be much too big for someone in current times to tackle alone.

Years ago, women joined orders that were near where they lived. Many joined the teaching orders that were active in the schools they had attended as children. Being in the South, there were no nuns in schools in the area. With current technology, orders were recruiting from all over the world through Internet communication. Transportation to various areas no longer presented a problem as we now had jets and other, easier means of transportation. The possibilities were limitless. Due to technology, recruiting for religious orders had taken a drastic change for both the orders and the inquiring women. This change would eventually hurt both the orders and the inquirers. It could lead some of these women into unexpected poverty, solitude, with no place to turn; much like those people whom they were initially drawn to serve.

Although I felt alone, I knew I wasn't. God wouldn't ask me to go anywhere without Him. So, together we began this journey that would lead me to the place where I could serve Him and His church. My entire life would be for the benefit of others. There was a great peace in just knowing I had said yes. I wanted to continue this journey of transformation, seeking a life of holiness, prayer, and service...or so I thought. I was unprepared for the darkness that lay ahead, a darkness that would swallow my whole life and test my faith beyond belief.

I started my search. I began simply by requesting information from the magazine, *Vision*. I carefully selected three different orders, requesting that more information be mailed to me. The magazine was a recruiting tool representing orders all over the world, and they specifically stated that one should check only three orders. It was a way to see their locations and learn of their ministries. As I patiently waited for information to arrive, I was quickly overwhelmed at the amount of material being delivered every day. At times, my mailbox was filled to the top, crammed full with letters, videos, and magazines. It was a battle just removing them from the box.

My phone rang off the hook, overloading my answering machine with messages from vocation directors. *What? How did all these people get my phone number?* I specifically asked for information on three orders. I felt as if I were nothing more than bait.

My heart felt heavier than ever, wondering if I would ever survive this process. I was a fish in a pond, waiting to be hooked for life by overbearing vocation directors. The search proved to be a long, drawn-out process that was draining me both physically and emotionally. My name seemed to be placed on hundreds of mailing lists. I even received information from France. They must have thought I was wealthy, with the ability to jump on a plane and visit France every month. The money spent on postage alone made my stomach queasy. I began to see each stamp as a bowl of rice never making it to a hungry child. The images of starving children seemed to consume my thoughts throughout the months to come.

I could not escape a recurring nightmare of dark-skinned children, with little clothing, in a dirty neighborhood. Their reflections were so vivid in the puddle of murky water they stood behind. Over and over again this image would haunt me while I slept and while I was awake. I couldn't escape it.

I emptied my mailbox every day. Otherwise, there would be no room for important mail such as bills and junk mail. The junk mail, which I once opposed, was a welcomed sight at this point. At least it drew my attention away from religious orders, even if only for a brief moment as I walked the long haul from my mailbox to my apartment. There was no escape from the stress and anxiety created by the overwhelming daily walk to my mailbox.

I resorted to tossing all correspondence into a large box and, at my convenience, I would read, discard, and sort through the pile of wasted paper and money. I was so overwhelmed by the sight of this enormous box, I was eventually driven to dragging it into the closet just to remove its painful sight. Day after day, I took a handful out and began sorting through the endless pile of solicitations. The original box was then replaced by three smaller boxes. One was for total rejection. It was one less possibility to consider. Although it did not physically decrease the weight of the box, it was incredible how just one envelope decreased the weight on my heart. Another box represented a possible interest, and a final box represented a strong desire to get to know more about them.

As the process concluded, I ran to the dumpster with the box of eliminated orders, forcefully tossing them in, as if to release some of the pain they had caused me. It was a great act of healing, which seemed to be the first step of encouragement. Finally, after approximately two years, the day arrived when all three boxes had been eliminated.

The process of elimination left me with information on three orders. Ironically enough, I had selected three orders...the three from which I had originally requested material.

CHAPTER 8

COME AND SEE

As time went on, I began visiting two of the three orders. I went to my first Come and See Retreat at the order that was closest, taking into consideration the cost of travel to the other two. Yes, I loved the area and the presence of God at this order. I felt so comfortable in the setting of this life. I was still, however, battling some more specific things. I wasn't quite ready to give up certain things yet, such as sleeping in on Saturday mornings. The big sacrifices didn't bother me; it was the little things creating the biggest tug-of-war.

I kept my process of exploration mostly to myself, with the exception of a couple of close friends and, of course, my parents. Only some people needed to know where I was on the weekends, and I didn't want to create any unnecessary rumors of mysterious weekend get-aways. At this time, however, I would have preferred rumors of this sort as opposed to rumors of my becoming a nun. I wasn't ready to face being ridiculed for my possible decision. I had years of discernment ahead of me, and I really didn't want too many voices in my discernment process... not until I had sorted through the hardest steps myself. When the time was right, when I thought I would be able to handle outside opinions, then I would let others know of my desire to serve God in a religious life. I kept my cell phone with me at all times in case my son called. At this time, he did not need to know where I was or what I was doing, as his life was consumed with protecting us as he served his tour of duty with the Marines.

At the end of the Come and See Retreat, a couple of other girls and I were invited to come back to another, smaller retreat the following weekend. CNN had requested the order to participate in a documentary on *The Decline of Women Entering Religious Life*. I was interested. I loved CNN, and I definitely wanted to know more about why there was a decline of women entering religious life today. Little did I know, this answer could not be uncovered by reporters through a special broadcast. Yes, CNN touched on the topic, broadcasting the obvious consequences of religious life, the inherent decline of the numbers of sisters over the years due to aging, and the low numbers entering today, but they failed to give any reasons for this decline. It would take many years of actual participation in the daily life within the orders to understand the complicated answer to this question.

It was a wonderful weekend, and the cameramen videotaped hours and hours of coverage. Everyone was as natural as could be expected, and short individual interviews were recorded. I answered the questions honestly, sure that the number of people who would actually watch a documentary on *The Decline of Women Entering Religious Life* would be very limited. It would probably be broadcast at an odd time, when most people were not even watching television anyway. I was comfortable with the thought that very few people would even see it, still hoping for privacy about my entering a religious order.

During one of the sessions, the topic arose regarding our willingness to discuss our choice to enter religious life with other people. The cameramen up until then were like flies on the wall. They went unnoticed, as if invisible, making no sounds whatsoever. It was at that point I realized that I, like most of the others, was not ready to talk to anyone else about my decision. It was a difficult topic, one met with various responses from acceptance to being totally cut-off from family and friends. It was at that very moment, when I was asked this question, that my thoughts flowed into words...very slow thoughts of total understanding at that point. I slowly began to speak, "Yes, I too, have a fear of telling others. Not knowing how to tell them; not knowing when the time is right; fearing their response to my decision of entering religious life." I became silent and turned my eyes to the cameramen, speaking directly to them, and stated, "I guess you guys will take care of that for me!" Laughter broke out throughout the room. It was like an icebreaker for the cameramen, who up until that time, seemed uncomfortable in this setting of serenity, silence, and prayer surrounded by only women. We no longer had to prepare a way to inform others of our decision. We only had to tell them to watch a documentary on CNN. They would do it for us.

The weekend came to an end, and we were to be notified of the date the interviews were to run. I received a phone call on a Friday night before St. Patrick's Day. It was the vocation director, "I'm sorry for such short notice, but CNN is running the program tonight at 9 p.m. on channel 25!" I scrambled. That was fifteen minutes away! I only had basic cable, with no more than a dozen channels. Therefore, I quickly called my parents and then flew over to their house, arriving precisely at 9 p.m. When I came in, Dad announced that Channel 25 is *Headline News*, and we must have gotten the wrong information regarding the channel. He pulled out the newspaper and checked the entire night's schedule. There was no documentary scheduled on any channel for the rest of the night. Although I was disappointed, I accepted the fact it must be on a sister station in the city where it was taped.

As we were talking, *Headline News* started to broadcast something about St. Patrick's Day and then... "Coming up next... The Catholic Church is facing a crisis today." We were silent. *What?* On *Headline News*! Everyone watches CNN *Headline News*. I began to feel the shock run through my body. Here it was being broadcast on *Headline News* on a Friday night at 9 p.m. I couldn't believe the number of hours taped just to get a short broadcast. It almost seemed like a waste of time for less than a five-minute segment. After we watched it, I went home, as we were celebrating the Sacrament of First Reconciliation the next morning with the children I was teaching. I didn't feel too anxious about it. After all, how many people would actually have seen a five-minute clip at that time of the night? I was sure...not many. I had convinced myself that most people were either out or watching movies on television.

The next day, I was approached by parents stating that they had seen the news that morning. *What?* "It ran last night. You mean you saw it last night?" "No," they replied, "we saw it at 6 a.m. this morning." Others announced the times when they saw it...11 p.m....7:30 a.m. CNN *Headline News* repeats its news all day long, every thirty minutes for those who want a quick update in a short period of time. I had thought it only ran as a filler the previous night, but it was still running and continued to run until midday. It was funny that everyone had seen it, but inside, I felt sick. *Would this ever cease?*

As phone calls came in, I was forced to address the issue. It seemed more people commented on my hair, my dress, and make-up (or lack thereof) more than on the topic of religious life. It seemed I would be able to endure it after all. Even my priest asked me for my autograph. I began to realize that nobody was really taking me seriously. I was aware that I was not the prime choice for one entering religious life, but I had to do what God was asking of me. For the first time throughout this process, I began to doubt if maybe I had really not experienced any of it. *Maybe I was just crazy? Would anyone ever be able to take me seriously?*

During one of my visits with my spiritual director, I remember packing a small bag of clothes. I told him I needed an answer to a very important question. I made him promise to answer me honestly. After a long open heart-to-heart discussion on my part, recounting all that had gone on in my spiritual life and truly believing in everything from the bottom of my heart, I asked my question. I had studied psychology for three years, and I had to know the answer. "Am I crazy? Crazy people don't know they are crazy. Therefore, I packed a bag, and I trust you with my life. If you think any of this is not real, I will not go home. I will check myself into a mental hospital today, right now."

His response was one I didn't expect. "No, you are not crazy." I knew that all I had experienced was real. I must remember, however, those who are out of touch with reality also believe their experiences are real. I had to rely on someone who knew my spiritual life, someone who had walked with me, someone who knew my prayer life.

My journey would continue. I trusted my spiritual director's answer. I unpacked the bag when I got home and never doubted again. I trusted like never before and would go wherever God sent me.

Once the negative attention settled down, I went on to investigate another order, the one that I felt I was truly being called to join. Several years had passed since my initial communication with the vocation director of this order. Due to my circumstances, I felt the need to move very slowly. I wanted to make certain of my son's independence before making a commitment to serve God in such a way of total surrender.

The time had come to make my first in-person visit with the sisters in the deep South. I would finally meet the vocation director with whom I had been communicating for such a long time.

Although I was invited to stay at the retreat center run by the order, I chose to stay at a nearby motel about thirty miles away. I prepared myself with a good night's sleep prior to the day of introduction. I had been getting to know the vocation director through communications and was eager to finally meet her.

I was given the name of another sister to contact once I reached the retreat center. She would be the one to give me a tour and welcome me, due to an unexpected change in the vocation director's schedule.

I woke up early, grabbed a quick breakfast, and spent more time trying to decide what to wear than ever before. My choices were limited, as I only had a few extra outfits in my suitcase. I had to be myself. If they wanted to meet me, I would be true to myself throughout every step of the way. I wanted them to present their true selves to me. Therefore, I would do the same for them. If they rejected me for who I was, then so be it. I couldn't spend the rest of my life trying to be someone I am not capable of being. I chose a simple cotton jumper over a tee shirt. My favorite way to dress.

I enjoyed the forty-five minute drive by the bay, wondering if I had the right address. I had never heard of a convent on the bay. *Could I be lost?* The area was one of luxury rather than sacrifice. After finding a place to park, I pulled out my map and driving directions to verify the address. Yes, this was it.

It was beautiful. Not quite what I expected. I never expected a convent to be on the water with boats, skiers, and the sounds of motors grumbling in the bay. I was thinking, "If this is a life of sacrifice...well, sign me up today!"

I quickly regained composure and promised myself not to be judgmental, a problem I would have to battle throughout this trip. I walked up the sidewalk leading to the retreat center, reminding myself to bite my cheek every time I caught myself being judgmental.

I trembled as I raised my arm to knock on the door. I had put so much into this discernment process and feared what I would discover when the door opened. *Where would this door lead me? To a life of prayer? A life of service? A life of missionary work? A life of sacrifice, serving God while also serving the least of our brothers and sisters?* Darkness never entered my mind. Religious orders are part of the Roman Catholic Church in which they support and serve...or so I thought.

I knocked the first time. No answer. I began to think of the percentage of elderly sisters in most orders. *Was this true for this order? Was the nun elderly and struggling to get to the door? Would she be using a walker to assist her? Why wasn't anyone coming?*

From Shadows of Darkness to Silhouettes of Hope

I bit my tongue. Do not jump to conclusions, I thought. Be open. Do not judge. I heard a voice from the other side of the door. It sounded like a telephone conversation. Yes, she was running the front desk and couldn't get off the phone. Finally, I heard the door unlock. My stomach seemed to turn a complete flip as the doorknob turned. This was it. *Did the door to my future just unlock? What will it hold for me?* I had been looking forward to this trip for weeks. I had hoped they were just as excited to meet me.

"Hello, can I help you?" the sister questioned in a computer-tone voice.

I eagerly announced, "Hi! My name is Dorothy, and Sister Grace is expecting my visit today!"

"Doris? Oh, yeah, she did say someone would be stopping by today." She invited me in and asked me to wait in the hall.

"My name is Dorothy, and I drove down from Alabama." I was surprised as my thoughts raced through my head. This trip was so important. I had a scheduled time to arrive, and I was to spend the entire day here. I didn't drive all that way to just "stop by." I bit my tongue. I would be polite. It seems that she just didn't know the whole story and how difficult it had been to even get here.

As I began to sit down, an older sister approached me. She asked me questions and immediately began telling me what a difficult life this was. As I looked around, I thought to myself, "If she only knew the sacrifices I was making just to drive here." Ouch, once again I had to bite my tongue. I began to pray as I listened to her tell of her sacrifices in this difficult life. God entered within and my words seemed to be not my own as I responded, "God said, 'Follow me.' He didn't say, 'Follow me, it will be easy.' " I was astonished at the words coming from my mouth as I knew they were not my own. The sister, whose face was one of shock, stopped her dialogue. There was an uncomfortable silence. She finally stated, "I guess you are right." The visit immediately took a turn for the worse as she quickly excused herself. So, I was really doing well. No one could seem to remember my name, and I had already offended a nun. I asked if I could visit the chapel while I waited. I needed some quiet time and didn't want to start any more conversations at that time. I decided it would be safer for me to just be quiet. I was already annoyed that anyone living in such a beautiful place (that had been donated to them by a benefactor) would ever complain about a difficult life.

The chapel was simple, surrounded by glass, and overlooked the bay. It was peaceful and offered a beautiful spot for a retreat. The boats, people, and sounds seemed to drift away as I was embraced by God's presence in this beautiful place.

Another nun, Sister Elizabeth, entered the chapel and introduced herself to me. She stated there was a silent retreat being held for a large group of people, and I would need to avoid conversation with any of the visitors. I was happy to hear that as I knew I would be better off in silence...at least according to my track record thus far.

Due to the silent retreat, we ate in a small room off the dining area so we could talk. Sister Elizabeth and I sat down as she announced one of the brothers would be joining us. I was pleased, because as I wanted to meet as many people as I could on each visit. The conversation began very slowly, and I felt it was a little uncomfortable. Brother John arrived and began to talk about football. I was hoping the conversation would develop into something a little more interesting, as I was not able to contribute to the conversation at all. I was feeling uncomfortable. They didn't know what to say to me. Maybe sports was just a safe topic.

Brother John finally realized the conversation was being monopolized by the two of them, and I was beginning to feel as if maybe they were just babysitting...an unwanted job taking up their Saturday afternoon. Brother John addressed a question to me. It was, of course, one that I hesitated to answer. I felt I was being taken to the edge of temptation, wherein I wanted to lie. "Do you like football?" he asked. How could such a simple question feel so complicated under this stress? "No, I really don't know all the rules enough to enjoy it." I saw the blank look on their faces, as if they had never met anyone who didn't like football. I quickly added, "But I love halftime and hotdogs!" Finally, the ice was broken. I was being me, the whole truth and nothing but the truth!

Laughter consumed us, and we couldn't contain ourselves. The kitchen door opened and a "not-so-happy" sister stuck her head through the small opening. We were reminded that there was a silent retreat being held, and we would have to hold it down. She glanced at me, and I immediately knew she suspected that I was the cause of such a disruption. Well, maybe I will fit in after all. They seemed to need a little laughter around here, anyway.

The day progressed, and Sister Elizabeth and Brother John quickly pulled me away from the silent retreat by taking me outside. Sister Grace, the vocation director, finally arrived, and I was very comfortable by now. She stated, "I heard you met Brother John." I felt the need to apologize immediately for our outburst. She laughed, and it, too, was an icebreaker.

I left with a peaceful feeling, knowing the experience was one of grace. I looked forward to the first Come and See Retreat, which would be held at another convent by the hospital, where several sisters worked. The drive home was filled with silence, soft music, and pleasant thoughts as I embraced the possibility of serving God with my entire being. There were actually people out there with the same desires I had. I couldn't wait to meet more.

Time passed by quickly. The next retreat, the Come and See Retreat, approached quickly. I had to fly to this retreat, since there was not enough time to drive. Sister Grace picked me up along with another interested young woman, Andrea, whom I had already gotten to know through correspondence. I was excited to meet her, since we had been communicating through Internet and telephone for several months. Finally, there was someone closer to my age, although she was in her early thirties and I was in my early forties. I was beginning to wonder if anyone was even close to our ages, but at that time, there were still so many more sisters to meet. Therefore, it was not yet a serious concern. After that first introduction to Andrea, we were like two peas in a pod. We were so much alike and spent a great deal of time getting to know each other that weekend. It was a great comfort to finally meet someone younger who had the same desire to embrace a life of prayer and service with their whole being.

We quickly gathered luggage and headed to the convent by the hospital. Wow, another beautiful, huge modern convent! We were shown to our rooms and then given a quick tour. One would have expected simple bedrooms with a twin bed, dresser, and desk with a lamp. The rooms were decorated more like home with each displaying our names on the doors.

I was surprised to discover an outdoor swimming pool. Andrea and I looked at each other, offering a questioning smile. *A convent with a pool?* It seemed we were the ones living lives of sacrifice rather than the sisters.

Both of us were struggling financially to meet the requirements. Andrea had moved in with her sister, living in a one-bedroom apartment, sleeping on the floor in an effort to become debt-free. Her meals consisted largely of pork and beans. I, too, had downsized to a one-bedroom apartment with no frills. I was trying to minimize my debt, which at that time seemed to be an impossibility. Yes, I felt as if we were the only ones living a life of sacrifice and poverty.

The retreat progressed and many different sisters offered their vocation stories of how they entered the order. There were no dramatic stories. The older sisters seemed to share the same story of entering right out of high school and receiving their college education through the order. Things had changed for the order since those days. At this time, you must have at least two years of a college education prior to entering. This, of course, meant almost every younger woman at the retreat had massive education debt that must be paid in full prior to entrance. The older ones had debt built up just from living expenses. Looking around, it would be years before any of us could actually enter due to the financial responsibility. It's obvious that this IS definitely one of the reasons there is a decline in religious life. There was no pressure, and everyone was comfortable knowing we were there only for information. After all, I was only in the "inquiring" stage.

We sat in a circle, listening, talking, and exploring. I was older than most of the others and did more listening than speaking. After all, I had already spent so much time getting to know the vocation director, and some of the group had just arrived for the first time. I wanted to hear everyone's stories.

As I flew home, my thoughts were consumed with the weekend. I had come to the conclusion that I had been judgmental. I had judged the young girl with her hair painted red. I had judged the girl who slept on the floor in the chapel. I had judged the older sisters who told their stories of entering the order right out of high school, because the choices offered back then were either marriage or religious life. If they didn't want to get married, they chose the convent. Yes, I caught myself judging once again. On the other hand, I was so drawn to their ministries, so drawn to the opportunity to attend mass every day, to have a chapel right in your own house, and to serve every day, seven days a week. Yes, this life was becoming the ideal way to live for me.

The weekend was over. It was time to jump back into reality. I must return home and get back to work, focused on getting out of debt. I needed to continue my spiritual direction and also contact more orders. I must do this for myself. I must be sure this is really for me.

As the plane rose above the clouds, I felt as if God Himself was holding me in His hands. I knew everything was going to be fine. Christopher was independent and living across the country.

I knew I wanted to be single the rest of my life but wanted to share my life with others. Although I loved being single and living alone, it was not something I wanted to do forever.

I closed my eyes, embracing the thought of entering the chapel every morning and every night for the rest of my life. I dreamed of receiving the Eucharist, my strength, every day until I reached my final destination. That which was once a dream was now becoming a possible reality.

CHAPTER 9

ACCEPTANCE

Finally, I applied for acceptance into the order. If accepted, it would take two years for the initial stage of discernment due to my financial situation and my inability to make monthly out-of-state trips. Each stage of acceptance was to be written and submitted for approval by the vocation board.

I was accepted by the order and began putting my plan into action, which was obviously not working. No matter how hard I tried, I could not get rid of the debt. My travel plans with work were not working out, because the order didn't have sisters where I was traveling.

Andrea was having just as much trouble as I was. Together we both decided that maybe everything was not going to work. I quit trying to force it. I went to the church, knelt before the cross, and turned it all over to God. There was no possible way I could do this alone. My prayer was from the heart. "I truly believe this is where you want me. Once again, there are impossible barriers to break down. If you really want me to go, break down the barriers for me, pave the way, and I will follow."

It was a great time of trust as I continued to work on my reading assignments, prayers, and my own personal studies. I was never without a pile of books, whether at home or on the road. The more I moved away from trying to do it all myself, the more God provided opportunities. I was now traveling quite extensively, and opportunities were quickly developing for ways of contact with other parts of the order.

I was in awe as I watched God's hand take over. I then began to really work on my budget. If God was doing His part, I must do mine. He suffered greatly for me, and in comparison, this was nothing. I cut my food budget down to nearly nothing, applying every penny to pay off debt. The more I sacrificed, the faster God worked.

The first year went by quickly, and Andrea applied for candidacy. I still needed another year. I wasn't going to enter as soon as Chris turned twenty-one. I needed at least one more year to be certain of his independence and more time to solve financial issues. Andrea was accepted and would be moving to the formation house in August of 2004. I would follow in August of 2005. It appeared that Sue, another interested candidate, would also enter at that time. I was thankful that I would not be entering alone.

Most of our contact was with the Southern sisters, but my travel would allow me to get to know the Northern sisters, as well.

Work quickly took me to a state up north. It was during this trip that I thought about searching for a homeless shelter run by one of the sisters, Sister Marie. I was staying in a motel in a tourist section, and it seemed that nobody had ever heard of this homeless shelter. I thought one of the police officers, with whom I was working, would know the next day. The officers were not aware of the shelter's location. One of the officers said, "Honey, this is a huge state. It could be hundreds of miles away. Don't get your hopes up."

I couldn't get it out of my head and stayed awake that night until I finally pulled the phone book out and looked the shelter up. Lo and behold, there was a listing under the name I was given. It didn't state what type of business it was, therefore, it could just be a coincidence. I thought it would probably just be a store, and if I called, an answering machine would pickup, confirming my belief.

From Shadows of Darkness to Silhouettes of Hope

After dialing the number listed, a voice answered after only two rings. Looking at my watch, I was quick to apologize for calling after midnight, identified myself, and explained my bizarre search for a homeless shelter run by Sister Marie. "Yes, this is it. You have the right number. I will tell her you called and suggest you call back tomorrow. She will be out until 2:00 p.m. Call back then."

Hanging up, I forgot to ask their location. I had the street address but no idea where it was. I couldn't sleep the rest of the night. At least I had made contact and would talk to another sister from the order tomorrow.

Work was busy, and I did not have a cell phone at the time. Borrowing my boss's phone, I had someone cover for me while I slipped out of the building to make my call. The phone rang, and I asked for Sister Marie, who came back to the phone with, "Hello Dorothy, I'm so glad you called back." Wow, at least she got my name right, and I hadn't even told her who I was yet. I was surprised when she told me she wasn't very far from my motel. She gave directions for me to meet her that night after dinner. "Oh, it's just down the road a few blocks. You can cut through the bus station, go out the back door, down a couple of blocks, and you're there."

I went back to work, excited about my discovery. I told a co-worker of my evening plans, and he wanted to accompany me to the shelter. He was a part-time Methodist minister, interested in the shelter, and thought it best I not go alone.

By the time we got on the van to go back to the motel, everyone was excited about their plans for the night. The minister was so excited about an opportunity to go to a famous football stadium that he had never been to before. As I announced I was going to visit a homeless shelter, I got looks of disbelief and a look of shock from the minister who, in his excitement of this great opportunity, had already forgotten his plans to accompany me on my adventure to visit the homeless shelter.

As I spoke, it was as if someone had hit him with a brick. His lapsed memory suddenly jarred him, and with extreme pain on his face, he stated he would go with me, apologizing profusely.

"This is a chance of a lifetime for you. Go, have fun, and I will be fine. After all, it's just down the road. I will allow ample time, and I have good directions." I insisted he go to the field. I would never stand in the way of this opportunity for him.

We unloaded the bus, gathered around for a quick briefing about safety, and were given limits in which we could roam. The officer informed us to keep our work badges on us at all times. If we had any problems, show the police our badges, and they would take good care of us. He told us not to go outside of the bounds set for our own safety. We were warned not to go near the bus station. As we listened to the boundary limits, we silently looked at each other, knowing without words being spoken, I was going beyond these limits. There was no stopping me.

One of the instructors insisted I take her cell phone. I made them promise not to tell. I had come this far and wasn't going to cancel just because it was a couple of blocks outside of the safety limits.

I grabbed something quick to eat and headed out for my journey, allowing an extra hour. It was very cold, and Sister Marie had said it was only a couple of blocks. I realized there was a huge difference in my definition of a block and hers. It was much farther than I ever expected. In fact, it was more like ten blocks. I had to walk very fast, as I knew I would be late if I continued to stroll, taking in all the sights. Finally, making it to the bus station, which was more like an airport, I slowed down. Running was not an option at this point. There were people all over the place.

Slipping into a restroom, I wondered why we weren't allowed to come here? There were homeless people, but it was a safe place for them. If I were homeless, I would come here, too. There was food, water, and shelter from the cold. I wanted to stay but had to keep moving. It was getting late, and I had not even found the back door yet. Finally, I found a door that looked like something I shouldn't enter. It was very dark and isolated outside. Surely Sister Marie wouldn't send me into a dark alley! Turning to a stranger for help, I trusted their information that the door led to a back alley and eventually to the street I was trying to find. I could cut across the vacant lot to save time and cut out a whole block. I thanked the stranger.

I hesitantly put my hand on the cold bar. I pressed it slowly, as the bitter wind was forced through the small crack. While I worked up the courage to step outside, I found a pitch black alley that led to a vacant lot. The vacant lot led to a dark street with no lights in sight. The awareness of the potential danger took my breath away. I reached into my pocket, feeling for the cell phone and badge. I wouldn't let fear stop me, although it had quite a grip on me at that time. Sister Marie had instructed me to walk straight, head up, like I knew what I was doing and where I was going. Forgetting those instructions, I ran like a bat out of hell.

As I ran, I was wishing I had chosen tennis shoes over black boots, which were now getting heavy, along with the weight of my long winter coat. At least my boots didn't have high heels, as I would have surely broken at least one of them off by now. I was thinking I should have worn something a little more casual. After all, I was going to a homeless shelter. *How could I have been so stupid?* I was standing out like a sore thumb, running through a dark alley in a deserted neighborhood. *Where were the police anyway?* If I were an officer, I would have stopped someone who was running like the wind through a deserted neighborhood.

As I spotted the building, I thought to myself, "This doesn't look like a shelter." Sister Marie was right. You would never know it was a homeless shelter. There was a very small sign above the door, and if you didn't know it was there, you would probably miss it.

It was dark. Very dark. I glanced at my watch, 7:00 p.m. Right on time. Good thing I allowed an extra hour. I knocked very loudly as I didn't want to linger outside any longer than necessary. The door quickly opened, and I was immediately welcomed in by a woman with a Southern accent. Ah, what a welcoming sound coming from her warm, smiling face. I was overdressed with my wool pants and sweater, but my only alternate choice was a work uniform.

Sister Marie and I spent some time getting to know each other upstairs in her office. The borrowed cell phone I had kept beeping, as messages were being left on my coworker's answering machine. Not knowing how to operate her phone, I chose to hang my coat downstairs by the door. Little did I know, it was my coworkers trying to find me...they felt I had been gone too long!

What an awesome ministry! I was given a tour of the facility, which was at least four or five stories high, including a commercial kitchen. There was an immediate connection, and I felt so comfortable here. Sister Marie had started this ministry herself, taking the chance, knowing it was what God was asking of her. The shelter was helping so many women to get back on their feet while giving them the confidence and skills necessary to succeed.

After the tour, Sister Marie introduced me to the fifteen residents seated in the dining room. I was also introduced to a sister from another order, who worked in the shelter. I quickly realized that I could not identify anyone. It was not what I expected. These people did not look like homeless people. If I didn't know who was whom, I wouldn't be able to identify who was homeless and who was not. They all had a story. They were real people who had fallen upon unexpected circumstances, which had left them in this situation. As I listened to the stories, I came to an unexpected, eye-opening awareness. This could very well be me. Some had lost jobs. Some had been evicted from their homes and had nowhere to turn. Some had lost their children by the time they came to the shelter, after trying desperately to keep them. Some were dealing with addictions that led to the loss of their home. Although they each had a different story, they all had one thing in common...they didn't plan it.

The Southerner was the woman who ran the kitchen. She was once a resident of the homeless shelter and decided to stay on as an employee. What a wonderful woman who made the choice to give back to those who helped her during her time of need.

I walked out that door a completely different person from when I walked in. I walked back to the motel in silence and with no fear. Homeless people are not to be feared.

As I walked back, I went through the very large bus station again, not only one time, but two more times. I loved it. People were everywhere, and I blended in like a grain of sand on a beach. Nobody cared what you did or what you said. I smiled at the homeless. They smiled back. God's grace is outside the bounds set by humans. I realized I must be cautious, but not fearful. I would never let fear keep me from the experience of God's grace in situations lying outside the boundaries we so frequently set.

I quickly got back on the street forgetting the time, embracing God's presence in the people to whom I was graciously introduced. I walked back slowly, contemplating what I had just experienced. I had met one woman who had given her entire life to benefit others in need of physical and emotional care. She had done this in an effort to give them back a life which they so richly deserved. Yes, I wanted to be a part of this.

As I continued my journey with this order, I was beginning to think about where I would do my live-in experience, an opportunity to actually live the life of a sister following their daily routine. It was assumed that I would ask for an area in the South, but I wanted a complete experience. I wanted to step outside the box. I wanted to experience God's grace to it's fullest potential. Therefore, I asked to complete my live-in-experience in the depressed areas of the Caribbean, where there was a presence of not only their order, but many religious orders choosing to serve in unfortunate economic areas.

One of my co-workers provided the trip for me with her frequent flier miles. This helped complete my requirements prior to entrance. I had no fear of going alone, although once Andrea heard I was going, she quickly made plans to join me. She had not completed her live-in experience either, and her entrance date was just around the corner.

The Caribbean sisters were different. They appeared to be more traditional. It was an experience of a lifetime, one that also changed me forever.

I didn't visit the tourist attractions. I went deep into the heart of the island, where the natives lived and avoided the small designated areas set aside for tourists. I loved the Caribbean culture, their school systems, and the poorest, forgotten areas in which few people ever venture. The mission for the poor was run by one sister who traveled in a van serving the needs of all.

I found the sisters were actually pulling out of the schools. Many of these schools only had the presence of one sister, and some sisters were planning on leaving other schools at the end of the year. I could see the order was not flourishing, but rather diminishing in the Caribbean. I also had the opportunity to spend time with another order, which had a great spirit, a traditional background, and a strong desire to serve the poor. They shared their stories with me, and I found a unique difference. Their experiences were different, their sacrifices heartfelt, and their call to follow God was illuminating.

My time in the Caribbean was the most dramatic transformation that I have ever encountered. It is not until you have held a woman in the final stages of Acquired Immune Deficiency Syndrome (AIDS) in your arms that you realize the power of prayer. It is while holding a skeleton with nothing more than skin clinging to her bones and a head gracefully resting in the palm of your hand, with eyes bulging in pain, asking for nothing more than prayer for her soul, that you find a depth of faith, a depth of love, and a depth of eternal and everlasting peace right here in the land of the living.

From Shadows of Darkness to Silhouettes of Hope

    It is not until you have hugged a man who was left for dead, with open knife wounds and dismantled body parts, one who had given up on life himself, that you can truly experience the healing power and miraculous love from a simple hug.

    It is not until you have listened to the stories of the poor who fish for their dinners, sharing any catches of the day with their neighbors on the street who have nothing to eat, that you truly know the meaning of charity.

    It is not until you live and love with the poor that you can truly understand the gift of faith. Yes, I had to leave this wonderful island in the midst of the Caribbean. What a beautiful place, what beautiful people, what beautiful faith!

    Oh, yes, I cried when I had to leave. I had so much more to learn from them. If you truly want to grow, if you truly want to be transformed, you must step out of your comfort zone. God's grace is outside the box, outside the boundaries we set for ourselves.

    It was weeks later before I finally got my pictures developed from my visit to the Caribbean. As I was browsing through the photos, I temporarily froze at the sight of one particular image. The image of dark-skinned children, gathered in front of a puddle...just like the image I could not remove from my mind, from years ago. It took my breath away as I noticed the reflection of the children in the murky puddle. I remember the day vividly. We were driving down a dirt road, when we came upon several very young children playing. There seemed to be no adults around as they played in the mud. I quickly jumped out of the car to ask permission to take their picture. The children quickly gathered around me with big smiles. I took the picture and quickly jumped back into the car, to escape the foul odor of sewage.

    The dream that had haunted me for such a long time was lying right there, in the palm of my hand.

CHAPTER 10

PROCEED WITH CAUTION

As time went by, I began to have concerns about Andrea's phone calls. She now was living in the formation house as a postulant. I was continuing my final year of preparation. The postulant year is an intense year of focus, prayer, and continued discernment. Vows are not taken for approximately three years. At that time, the postulants are considered to be temporary, as discernment continues. The postulant year is to be a year of focus, knowing your time with family would be minimal during this period.

I was becoming concerned about Andrea's well-being, as I spoke with her from time to time during the first few months. She had concerns and, over a period of a few months, I began to notice negative changes in her, along with comments that were just not supporting our Catholic faith. She entered as a very loving and caring young woman who had a desire to know more about the Catholic faith. She had pointed out an interest in a book about the Liturgy of the Mass, stating that she had hopes of learning more about the meaning of the celebration of the Mass. I felt Andrea lacked the necessary knowledge to discern what is truly our faith. She was an ideal candidate for persuasion of distorted beliefs.

Andrea stated that her sister was coming for a visit for Thanksgiving, which I felt was a little unusual at the time. Visitors are not a common part of the postulant year. This was a Catholic Religious Order, and I knew they would have her best interest at heart. They would recognize any signs of anxiety or stress. I was sure she was just overwhelmed.

Andrea's spirits seemed to lift after her visit with her sister, easing my concerns. She spoke of the things they did together, and I felt a short-lived relief in her voice.

Andrea then began to voice concerns to me about strange things going on in the house. It was very hard for her to describe the situations. She stated that the situations were strange and abnormal. She stated that other people were being involved in these strange situations. She stated that she wanted to go home. I was shocked, to say the least, as she had sacrificed so much and for so many years to get to this point. I didn't understand what she was talking about. Not knowing what was going on, I was supportive of giving it time. I felt she might possibly be exaggerating. I felt that maybe Andrea needed someone in whom she could confide and receive the spiritual direction, which was promised to her prior to entering.

During one of Andrea's last phone calls to me, she told me that her parents were coming to the house for a visit. I felt this was highly unusual. She stated the formation director, the sister assigned to the postulants during this first year, invited them because she had asked to go home. The formation director convinced Andrea's parents that she was homesick and thought it would be good if they came to the formation house for a visit. I didn't hear from her for a while. I thought the visit from her parents might have been a positive experience, and all was well... until I received her very last phone call.

My phone rang, and when I picked it up, there was someone crying. I couldn't understand a word she was saying. "It's me, Andrea." She spoke in a low voice, as if she didn't want anyone to hear her. "I want to go home with my parents, and they won't let me," she sobbed.

"What? Your parents are back for another visit?" I knew then that something was not right.

"No, they're still here. They're leaving, and I told them I want to go with them." She was whispering, crying, and desperate. She stated that Sister Rachel, the formation director, was doing the same thing to her parents that she had been doing to her. Andrea desperately wanted to go home with her parents, but they had been in the house for a month and were now declaring she couldn't come home.

She then had to go and quickly hung up. That was it, the end of our phone call. I never heard from her again. Convents, no matter how relaxed, do not allow parents to come and visit for a month during the postulant year, or any other year for that matter. I knew this was not a normal circumstance. Worried about her well-being, I casually asked my vocation director about Andrea. I was told that she was doing well, and all updates were very positive. She convinced me about her well-being, I figured it was normal to keep your phone calls to a minimum at this time in your postulant year. I also decided Andrea must have been embarrassed by her previous phone call, in which the haunting word of "brainwashing" was used.

As time went on, I became acquainted with Ruth, another potential candidate, who was also considering religious life. It was obvious they would not accept Ruth, because of her knowledge, including a Master's Degree in Theology. There were power struggles at every visit. Ruth knew her theology. I remained silent. They did not know how much I knew about my faith.

During one of the retreats held at the formation house, Ruth spent hours talking to a very good friend of hers who was a priest named Adam. She and I were in a room discussing some of the beliefs she had observed. At that time, I had not witnessed anything more than a few caution flags. On the other hand, Ruth had spent a lot more time with the Northern sisters and had filled Father Adam's ears with much more information than I had access to. When I asked what Father Adam said to do, she replied, "He said get out, get out now, and don't go back!" I felt that was a little harsh and unfair as he was not there, and he had not received the information first hand. *How could this be true?* I didn't understand! This is a Catholic Religious Order, surely it was only Sister Rachel's distorted view of Catholicism or ideas. There is always one in the crowd, no matter where you go. I guess Sister Rachel could voice her opinions against some of the things the church does, but I also felt she shouldn't do it in front of us. It just wasn't right. After all, we were giving our life to the church in support of Rome, in support of the Catholic Church. After all, this is our faith.

As time passed, back in the office of the vocation director, the lay person working in the Vocation Department made a very strange statement against the sisters. She was very upset, stormed out, and never came back. She left with the words, "In the name of Jesus, every knee shall bend...It's all about Jesus!" She was upset with many of the practices the order was following. When she left, she took with her a manual that she was working on and never returned it. I thought this, too, to be pretty bizarre. Sister Grace, the vocation director, seemed to blame the lay person for her actions of storming out and taking the manual with her. Once again, I had two different stories and did not know the truth.

I had been trying to get answers to some questions, but they were never given. I remember Andrea tried to get the same questions answered and never did either. We wanted to know when the last person had entered the community. We never got an answer. We were finally given the information about other candidates entering the previous years. All of them went home for Christmas and never returned. They supplied reasons for each of them. I knew religious life was hard, and some people just couldn't take the sacrifices. That was not too alarming to me at the time.

All of these abnormalities that brought up caution flags were written off as one individual's interpretation or idea rather than the order's overall view. After all, this was a Catholic Religious

Order that was supposed to be accountable for their actions and to support Rome.

I knew religious life wouldn't be easy. There would be different people with different ideas. I just didn't realize there would be any conflict pertaining to our own faith. By the time any serious caution flags were raised, I had already been accepted into the candidacy program, sold my car, paid off my debt, and resigned from my job. My clothes were packed, shipped, and ready for my arrival. All of these tasks created a great deal of stress. I was required to carry all of this out one month prior to entrance. This gave me a month to adjust to the situations. I felt the stress and anxiety were causing unnecessary caution flags and brushed it off. I focused on the future year that would fill my desires for prayer, transformation, and serving. The final month was spent moving some of my belongings into a storage unit and discarding the rest.

I can honestly say I had never trusted God to such a depth. I knew without a doubt that this was where God wanted me. Whatever was to become of the caution flags would be part of His will, part of His plan. I wouldn't allow myself to question anything else. I had been involved with this order for seven years, and I would be able to handle any possible questions pertaining to our faith. God provided the way. This was important to Him. Therefore, it was important to me.

PART III

OBEDIENCE TO GOD

CHAPTER 11

THE FLIGHT

It was a hot August day when I boarded the flight that would change the direction of my life forever. I was seated by the window as I went over the checklist I had completed earlier that morning. Most of my belongings had been previously shipped. Personal documents, cell phone, and a small amount of money were all accounted for on the way to the airport. I was accustomed to traveling alone. Therefore, fear was not an emotion I had to deal with. I wasn't concerned that an unfamiliar sister would be picking me up. I had already programmed her cell phone number into my phone to alleviate any tension.

My mind was at ease as the plane lifted its wheels off the runway. The incline forced my head against the back of the seat. The engines seemed to be whining extra loudly, as they struggled to lift us up and over the clouds. The sun was bright, and its warmth allowed me to drift away from the noisy engines, which were still whining throughout the flight.

I thought of the apostles and how easy it seemed for them to drop everything and follow Jesus when He said, "Follow me." I recalled the past seven years of my own life. The doubts, struggles, sufferings, and detachments encountered over the years were a far cry from the apostles' journey. It didn't seem real. It seemed as if the past seven years were just a dream. After all, the barriers presented over the years seemed to be an impossible challenge. The years of preparation and sacrifice showed its face on a thin body, which had been pushed to its limits throughout this phase of discernment. I finally recognized the toll of this journey, coming to the full realization of God's grace, which had carried me to this point. I felt a sense of relief. My life of service was finally going to begin. The Lord had carried me through the biggest test of my life. I thought there was light at the end of this difficult road, and it was all worth it. Little did I know, the test which I thought was over had not even begun yet!

I was consumed with thoughts of my son. Chris had dedicated a portion of his life for our freedom...to protect and serve in a time of war. His sacrifice was so much greater than mine. We both entered into destinations of the unknown. Unlike his, however, I knew mine would be safe...or so I thought. My "yes" to serve was nothing compared to his "yes" to serve. I admired this young man so much. My son.

I reached into my purse, clutching the beautiful rosary beads Chris had given me for Christmas. I pulled out the card in which he had written a beautiful message. On the small envelope were the words "Mother/Dorothy." I opened the card for the thousandth time, I'm sure. "Wherever you go, and whatever you end up doing, know that I support you. Take this with you, and know that I will always be thinking of you. I love you more than you know, and I will always be with you. Merry Christmas. Love you, Chris." I stared at my name on the envelope and drifted over the past twenty-two years. I had completed the most important job of my life. Although I would always be there for him, I would have to let him make his own decisions now. He was a grown man with a big heart, and the world awaited his presence. I knew his journey would include the ups and downs of life in general. I also knew these mountains and valleys would be tools that would shape him into the person God created him to be.

I thought of my own mountains and valleys, which brought a smile to my face. A friend once told me, "You have lived a life from hell." I laughed and replied, "I wouldn't have changed a thing about my life. Every situation brought me to where I am today. Everything is for a reason. It's all part of God's plan."

Compassion doesn't just appear like magic. Compassion is born from pain. Pain from my own adult experiences allowed me to connect with the pain of others, enabling me to reach out and feel their circumstances. Inevitably, I realized that my own suffering was not as bad as the suffering of others.

These experiences continued to cycle, bringing about a deeper level of compassion for all God's children. People who were once nonexistent became the center of my vision. I couldn't escape it. I previously walked through life oblivious to God's suffering children; blind to their presence among us.

There is no way to explain how I see the world today. No matter how hard I try, there are just no words that describe it accurately. It's like the world is living in "color," and those who suffer are living in "black and white," standing out like a sore thumb. It's as though God had given me glasses that I could not remove.

There are so many reasons for the suffering. Sometimes it comes from a physical need, and sometimes it is a spiritual need. No matter the need, the consequences produced remain the same... great suffering. I have also found that suffering is a part of life. Sometimes the suffering can be eased, but sometimes it cannot. Even a brief moment of relief from suffering can help a person.

I recalled the cross that Jesus carried for us, and how He experienced a moment of brief relief when a cup of water was offered to Him. It was offered out of compassion, out of love. Sometimes our own acts of compassion are never received completely, just as Jesus never consumed the cup of water offered to Him. Although He didn't drink the water to alleviate His thirst, He felt the deep compassion of the person who reached out to Him.

Peace filled my heart as I returned the rosary and card back into my purse. I knew I would carry it with me everywhere I went for the rest of my life. It was Chris's courage that gave me the strength to say "yes" to God. This note was the final confirmation for me. Yes, I would go wherever God wanted me to go. My journey would have the same trials of mountains and valleys, successes and failures, but it would not lack compassion as I tried to relieve the suffering of those who lived in the "black and white" vision of my eyes. This rosary would always be a reminder of the Suffering, Death, Resurrection, and Ascension of our Lord. I knew the prayers said on this rosary would sustain me throughout my journey.

The reality of what I was doing started to set in as I thought about what I had given up over the past thirty days...a good job, medical insurance, a car, and a good portion of my personal belongings.

The one thing I did not have to give up was my family. Although I would be farther away, family visits would always be possible. Home assignments were also granted in times of family illness. This greatly eased any fear created by the thought of my absence during a serious family illness.

Family was important, and all the sisters talked about frequent family visits. I would not have made it this far without the support of my family. I was required to leave my job thirty days prior to entrance, in order to prepare myself gradually for the new life and routine that would soon follow. Financially unable to do this, my parents welcomed me back home for the month prior to leaving. I was very fortunate to have family support, a luxury many women do not have. I began to wonder how I would have made it without my family support. Once again, God had provided.

I reached into my purse again and pulled out my key ring. Resting in the palm of my hand was the proof of everything I had recently let go. My key ring, once heavy with keys for my apartment, work, and car, was nearly empty. There was only one remaining key, which had a white ribbon tied around the end. As I held the key to my heart, I was reminded of a going-away dinner held at a Japanese restaurant prior to leaving.

From Shadows of Darkness to Silhouettes of Hope

We had attended a vocation hour of prayer. I was asked to speak about my own journey. After the prayer service, my family, priest, and spiritual director went to dinner. I had been given a key to the church and, with all the chaos, had forgotten to return it. I removed the key from the keyring and handed it to the priest. I was surprised when he took it, looked it over, and handed it back with the words "Keep it with you and always know that you have a home here." It was comforting, and I accepted the key still tied with the white ribbon. The ribbon represented the presence of God and was a reminder, a concrete symbol, of His presence. He was with me in times of great joy and in times of great suffering.

I placed the key back into a zippered compartment in my purse for safety. Fumbling around some more, I pulled out a small note from one of the sisters I had met at another order while in the Caribbean. I read her kind words in the note of encouragement. "Yes, this is where God wants me to be," I thought to myself.

My mind drifted to the day I met this unique nun, Sister Mary Lin. She was one of the holiest people I had ever met. She had no concern for herself whatsoever but had such a great compassion for the poor and suffering. She had left her native country, knowing that she would never see her family again. I felt that my sacrifice was nothing compared to the depth of hers, which was one of great holiness. Every time I felt the weight of my own sacrifice, I would think of Sister Mary Lin, which lifted my heart completely.

Before I knew it, the plane was descending. We were soon flying below the clouds, preparing to land. The pilot reminded us to keep our cell phones off until the plane had come to a complete stop. We were not to use them until authorization was given. As he was speaking, I slipped my hand into my purse to locate my own cellphone, just for reassurance. It was my only way of contact with the sister assigned to pick me up at the airport. As I fumbled through my purse, I came to the realization that my phone was missing. My heart began to beat faster as panic began to creep in. I remembered having it in the car. *What had I done with it? Had it fallen out of my pocket?* There was no time to waste. The plane unloaded quickly.

I ran to the terminal of my connecting flight and dumped the contents of my purse onto the floor. No phone appeared in the small pile that stared at me from the floor. I realized how much my life had changed as I peered over the items. My purse didn't contain the items of a normal woman of forty-five years. There was no evidence of nail polish, make-up, jewelry, or electronic devices. The contents on the floor revealed a completely different woman, one whom many no longer recognized. I scooped up the pile, tossing everything back into my purse, and took off running to catch my next flight. I couldn't miss it. I had no means of communication at that point.

The next flight was not filled with thoughts of past memories or future possibilities. It was consumed with the present moment of fear and the lack of means for communication.

I survived the trip without a cellphone. The plane was on time, and I realized my dependency on technology was one that I would have to shed. A few days later, a package arrived, containing my cellphone. It seemed that my phone had slipped out of my pocket while riding to the airport. As I was frantically looking for my phone at the terminal, it was cruising back home in the backseat of my parents' car.

CHAPTER 12

ENTRANCE

I was ecstatic with my new experience of religious life. Visiting the chapel the first thing in the morning and the last thing at night would soon become a regular routine. Although I had attended daily mass prior to entering, it was now a guaranteed part of my daily life.

There would be no more sneaking down the stairs at work and slipping out of the office in order to attend mass. There would be no more rushing to avoid a late entrance to the daily chapel mass, which was held at the nearby Catholic school. I would inevitably lose my parking space, which was close to the building in which I worked. I was forced to run back to work from the only parking spot left...a good hike away. The frantic rush seemed to take away some of the serenity that normally followed every celebration of mass. Those days were gone. Finally, daily mass would be a regular and eagerly awaited part of my daily life.

I was given the opportunity to adjust and settle in for a couple of days prior to the entrance ceremony. The ceremony was held in our own chapel, located in the convent. It was simple, and sisters who lived in nearby areas attended both the ceremony and the following dinner.

The convent was a very large, two-story house with a basement. My bedroom consisted of a bed, a desk, a small closet, a dresser, and a sink. I was very thankful for the unexpected sink.

The bathroom was located down a long hall, which was lined with bedrooms once occupied by sisters. Today, with the decline of women entering religious orders, some of the bedrooms had been turned into offices. There were six women who lived at the convent. Some of the other bedrooms were used for guests during retreats. A trip to the shower could actually accomplish one's daily exercise routine. No items were to be left in the bathroom. Therefore, one shower often included several hauls up the hallway to retrieve forgotten items. I didn't mind at all. The extra trips were just considered a sacrifice for the great gift of daily mass.

I was consumed with happiness, and it showed. There was no hiding my love for this life. I was soon dubbed with the nickname "happy, happy, joy, joy" by Sue, the other postulant.

It seemed, I was told, that nobody could actually be that happy and filled with such joy. I was told I needed to be more myself...more "authentic." Knowing my joy was real, I thanked God for such a great gift and asked Him to fill Sister Rachel, the formation director, with an abundance of joy. I asked that she, too, would see this life as the gift it truly was. The other sisters had lived this life for such a long time. I felt that they were possibly taking their life for granted now.

We soon found ourselves searching for work in order to support and contribute to our room and board expenses. We had to consider the location of our employer due to the fact that there was only one car for the postulants (new recruits) to share. Although we both had an interest in working at the same Catholic organization, we were divided. I took a position at a Catholic church that was within walking distance. There were Catholic churches every few blocks up North. I wanted to experience as many Catholic churches as possible. Therefore, my day started early with a mile and a half walk to one of the churches for 6 a.m. morning mass. After the walk back to the convent, I had time for a quick breakfast before morning prayer, which started at 8 a.m. I then headed out for another church where I worked. This was approximately a two and a half mile walk to this Catholic church and their Catholic elementary school. The neighborhood was beautiful and in an exclusive part of town.

My day concluded with the same walk back to the convent. Dinner, chapel, and preparations for the next day were soon part of my regular routine every night.

I focused my thoughts on prayer, mass, work, and reading. We were soon attending theology classes with other orders, adding homework assignments to the already busy evening. I loved my life! My bedroom was directly above the chapel at the top of the stairs, next to the business office. I became friends with the lay woman in the office, and her daily smile was a welcomed gift.

Since there were only two of us in the formation process, there were other sisters living in the formation house in order to provide a way of living in a community. I already knew some of the struggles I would face, due to living in community. I accepted the challenges that would be placed before me.

I had finally completed my entrance for discernment. This was the beginning of my time to live the life of a religious woman and decide if it was really for me. I would be experiencing a life of total commitment to God, serving Him by serving His church. This was the faith that I loved with my entire being. I was willing to endure the welcomed growth of obedience and transformation, which would challenge me to live a life more closely conformed to His will. I would endure anything that enabled me to serve Him more completely.

There was only one thing that I was not prepared to endure...I had given my life to serve and support the Roman Catholic Church, not to fight it. There were issues raised at the formation house that did not follow the Catholic faith that I knew and loved. I was not prepared to accept a twisted, abnormal way to transform the views of my sacred faith to the distorted views of an unknown faith, which I was being persuaded to accept. The changes varied in disobedience from the refusal to accept liturgical norms set by Rome, to the support of activities of others that would result in excommunication from the Roman Catholic Church completely, and to the total distortion of scripture as taught by the Roman Catholic Church.

The process of transformation over the next three months would take me into the abyss of a very dark shadow to include manipulation, brainwashing, and isolation. Refusing to conform to this transformation, I would endure great suffering of the consequences.

I had given up too much for God not to follow His way. I would not allow my precious faith to become distorted. How could this have happened? This was a Catholic organization. I had never heard of groups that had drifted away from that which I wanted to serve. This religious order of women wanted the same power that priests had. They wanted to change the Roman Catholic Church. I was in total shock! *Would anyone even believe me? How could a Catholic Religious Order oppose the election of Pope Benedict XVI?* As time went on, I knew without a shadow of a doubt that there was no way of bringing them back to our faith. I was right in the middle of a spiritual battle... that powerful battle of Holy/Hell. Yes, evil exists. Anything that is not of God is evil. What I was experiencing was not of God. God is love. God's presence is known by the authentic gifts of the spirit...charity, joy, peace, patience, kindness, generosity, gentleness, faithfulness, and modesty.

I had given my life to God, to serve Him by serving and supporting the Catholic faith and all it stands for. I respected the beliefs for which Sister Rachel fought so strongly; beliefs that were contrary to the Catholic faith. We live in The United States of America. We have freedom of religion. There are people and denominations that agree with the same ideas that Sister Rachel embraced. I felt that Sister Rachel was free to leave the Catholic Church, attend seminary for another denomination, become a minister, and serve within that denomination.

I felt that Sister Rachel did not have the right to manipulate the thinking of another human being who gave their life to serve the Catholic Church. I had to consider my own soul. I could not be a part of bringing others into an organization presenting itself as something it was not. I could not be a part of tampering with vessels that God Himself had called to serve. I would be responsible for not only my soul, but all those I would mislead. Yes, I had all that I longed for...prayer, mass, and a life of service. Even though I had all that I longed for, I could not jeopardize my soul. I would rather suffer the loss of those things in order to preserve my faith and my soul.

I had no choice. I had to leave. After all, this was a time of discernment. I was not suited for this order. And then, the unexpected horror was placed before me...leaving was no simple task.

The darkest shadow began to consume me as I remembered the phone calls from Andrea. She, too, had wanted to leave. Instead of permission being granted for her to leave, her parents were brought in for an entire month. According to Andrea, the same twisted brainwashing process was used on them.

My goal was to escape this shadow that was taking every ounce of my being to fight. *Would its darkness consume my entire being? Would I be lost in this abyss of darkness for the rest of my life?*

CHAPTER 13

SUGGESTIVE THINKING

It was the third day of my new life, when the first flag of caution appeared. We were at the dinner table, and there was a conversation about the hot water problem in one of the showers. It seemed there was one shower that only ran boiling hot water, and I was to avoid it. There were only three showers in the bathroom. There was one full bathtub with a shower on the right, another full bathtub with a shower on the left, and a very small shower without a bathtub, also located on the left side.

Sister Rachel asked which shower I had used that morning. When I told her I used the shower on the left, she insisted I did not, because that was the one in need of plumbing repairs, and it only ran scalding hot water. She stated I would have gotten burned if I had actually used that one. There was no mistake in knowing which one I used. The first day, I chose the very small one. It was too cramped, so I used the full-sized shower on the left the next day. The other full-sized shower on the right had a sign on the bathroom door..."Do Not Use."

I knew which one I used, and I wasn't going to say I used another one. I was going to tell the truth, no matter what. "I took my shower at 4:30 a.m., before anyone got up. Maybe there was cold water in the pipes, which cooled it down," I suggested.

Sister Rachel made me leave the dinner table, taking me upstairs to point out the one I used. I calmly pointed to the full-sized shower on the left. I showed her where I had placed my clothes. I then pointed to the full-sized shower on the right with the "Do Not Use" sign on the door. "See, this one has the sign on it. It says 'Do Not Use.' Therefore, I did not use it." I walked over to the tiny shower stating, "This was the one I used on the first day, but it was so cramped that I decided to use a larger one." I also apologized, asking if we had assigned showers to use. I was afraid I had possibly used hers and might have upset her. She verified that we could use any shower we wanted, but this one would scald me. She would not stop. She wanted me to give in, admitting I had used a shower that I really had not used. I remained silent. She insisted one more time that I wasn't telling the truth. I remained calm and spoke softly stating, "I am very sorry, but I know which shower I used." We returned to the dinner table to a plate full of cold food. I ate the cold dinner and prayed silently.

I wasn't sure what had taken place, but I knew what the truth was. I was not going to bend it. The next morning, I used the same shower. The water was fine. Sister Rachel claimed the plumber had come to repair it. I was home all day and never saw a plumber. I asked an office employee if she had seen a plumber, and she stated that she had not.

Why did this happen? What was the purpose for it? I lost several nights of sleep trying to understand the reasoning of such a bizarre situation. I could understand the situation being one of obedience if I had been assigned a shower and chose to use another one. This was not about obedience. I was not sure what this was about.

I remembered my keyring, the one that held the key to my church at home, the one tied with a white ribbon. I placed the key on my end table. I wanted the ribbon in sight, as a reminder that God was with me.

I tried to focus on my new job and ministry opportunities. Sister Rachel had turned her focus to Sue, the other postulant. It appeared that Sister Rachel was giving Sue a very hard time. Sue was becoming more distant toward me, even to the point of avoiding my presence.

It did not take long to accomplish the task of separating our lives completely. Sue and I very seldom had the opportunity to talk to each other alone. Therefore, I was eagerly awaiting the spiritual direction that I had been promised. We were to be given a choice of sisters from other religious orders once we settled in. I needed an objective person with whom to talk, one who could help me discern all aspects of the formation process. After all, this was a time of discernment, a time to live the life to see if it was right for me. It was also a time for the order to see if I would be suited for a life of service with them.

The opportunity for spiritual direction never came. When I addressed the question, I was told by the formation director that she would be my spiritual director.

Sister Rachel tried to manipulate my thoughts about Sue. I fought the manipulation by defending Sue, but I soon realized it was a battle that I would lose. I had knowledge about the group of girls who entered two years ago. They left at Christmas and never returned. It was obvious that the plan was created through communication with each other. Therefore, I understood their reasoning to divide us.

In order to accomplish this division, Sue and I were left in the house alone for a weekend. Oblivious to the manipulated scenarios ahead of us, I was looking forward to the opportunity for a private conversation with her.

We were each given a copy of our schedule, which contained our weekend assignments. Neither one of us thought to compare them. We had guests in the house for a private retreat, which created a more complicated situation.

The worse scenario came into play when all schedules contained a time for chapel prayer, except Sue's. After chapel, we were to work in the soup kitchen, located in another state. We had to catch a train by 8:30 a.m.

When Sue did not arrive for chapel, I went to locate her. She was eating breakfast and became very upset when she realized the difference in schedules. I asked her to come in and join us.

From Shadows of Darkness to Silhouettes of Hope

We would wait for her to finish breakfast. I told her chapel would be over in time to catch the train. We were to take the train first, transfer to the subway, and walk the remaining distance to the soup kitchen. We had only been there one time, and I was not sure I could remember the directions. Sue assured me that she remembered the way.

I had a responsibility to the guests to provide chapel. Sue never arrived. Although I did shorten the prayer service, I dared not skip it entirely.

As soon as we finished, I ran to the dining hall. Sue was not there. I ran up the stairs to her room. Sue was not there either. My heart sank, and my body became limp as I realized that she had left me. I could not believe she had really done that. I would never be able to remember the directions! The soup kitchen was in another state, and the subway was so confusing. I could not miss my assignment. I couldn't just give up. There was no time to waste. I had to go. I ran to the cabinet that held our train and subway tokens for the weekend. The envelope was gone! How would I ever get there? My heart sank once again. I couldn't believe Sister Rachel's manipulation actually put me in this situation.

I thought for a minute. I had slipped a ten dollar bill into my billfold for emergency money during my flight when I left home. Sometimes planes are delayed, and I might have needed a meal. It was all I had. Ten dollars would get me there, but I knew it was not enough to get me back home. I had to do it. I had five minutes before the last train was to leave, and it was at least a ten to fifteen minute walk to the train station. I didn't know if I would make it or not, but I had to try. I ran as fast as I could through town. When I got to the train station, I chose an attendant, rather than purchasing my ticket from a machine. I had no time for mistakes. "Has the train left yet?" I huffed. "It's about to leave. You might make it...run fast!" she stated. I ran as fast as I could to the loading dock. I slipped in just as the doors were closing.

I found the closest seat and collapsed. I looked around. There was no sign of Sue. *Did she take an earlier train? Did she actually go?* I was getting sick. Was she so mad that she didn't even go to her assignment? My mind began to race. I did not know how I would get back if Sue had not gone.

I had to watch for my destination. *What was my destination?* I didn't even know the station where I was supposed to get off. Sue knew the directions, and she wasn't here! Maybe I would recognize it. I watched with anticipation. They all were familiar, but I didn't recognize the one where I was supposed to exit. Then, there was a station I had never seen at all. I thought I must have missed it. My heart began to beat faster as I looked out the window. Finally, I saw something that looked familiar...I thought this might be the stop.

After saying a little prayer, I jumped off and began running. There was supposed to be a subway station nearby. There were people everywhere. I couldn't see through the crowds. I was getting pushed and shoved as people were moving so fast. They knew exactly where they were going, and I seemed to be in their way. I could not even find an attendant to help me.

I finally made it to a ticket booth. I was right. I had just enough money to get me to the soup kitchen. I looked at the amount of change in my hand. *How would I get home if Sue wasn't there? What if she didn't have the tokens with her? What if she had hidden them in the house?* My mind was racing with all these possibilities.

I couldn't waste any more time with worries. I had an assignment. I had to make it. Mass would be celebrated prior to serving lunch. I had to be there. Glancing at my watch, I doubted I would make it. I didn't even know where to get off the subway. Once again, I had hoped I would recognize the street. Finally, I saw familiar buildings as we approached the city. Now, to find the right stop. They all looked alike! Every stop was identical. I knew I would never be able to find the right one. I would have to just get off and ask directions.

From Shadows of Darkness to Silhouettes of Hope

As the subway slowed down, I got ready to run. I ran and ran and ran. It was a bad section of town with an incredibly high rate of crime. Once again, I found myself running in a dangerous city, not knowing where I was going. Only this time I had no money and no badge to protect me. In fact, I had no identification on me, whatsoever. What would I do if I couldn't find the soup kitchen? I was running so fast and nothing looked familiar. I stopped and asked people for directions. They did not know where the soup kitchen was. I saw a police woman enter a store about a block away. I ran, hoping she would still be in the store when I got there. As I pushed the door open, she was coming out. I stopped for a moment. This was my opportunity. Part of me wanted to ask for a ride to the station, to escape this bizarre, dangerous woman...Sister Rachel. I thought of Andrea. I thought of Sue. I couldn't just disappear. I had to stay. I had to find out what was really going on in this house of darkness; this house that was consuming me with a dark shadow.

The police woman asked, "Can I help you?" I quickly came to my senses and stated, "Yes, I'm looking for a soup kitchen. It's run by Catholics, and I don't have an address." She told me that they had a lot of soup kitchens in this part of town. I gave her as much information as I could possibly remember, and finally she pointed me in the direction of a soup kitchen that was very similar to the one I described. Although she did not know the exact address, she pointed me in the right direction.

I ran and ran and ran some more. At the point of collapsing, I asked directions from a group of what appeared to be homeless people. They said it was over a couple of blocks. I was down to five minutes before mass was to start. I couldn't breathe. My side hurt. I was cold. I was hungry. I was ready to give up, but I continued to run.

Finally, I reached the building. When I opened the door, I leaned against a wall, sliding slowly down to sit on the first step of a very steep flight of stairs. This was my next test. I thought to myself, "I cannot take one more step."

Leaning against the wall, gasping for air, I began to shed my coat. I could feel the heat from the kitchen. I was hot, sweating, and now nauseous from the smell of food. I needed water. I thought about just skipping mass. I thought about walking back out the door. I just didn't have the energy to walk up the stairs. I thought of the consequences. I heard the music begin. Finding a burst of energy, I ran up the stairs.

I collapsed in the first seat I saw. I hesitantly looked around for Sue. They had already begun the opening song. Under normal circumstances, I would have burst into tears by now. I had endured so much already that I was numb. And then, I saw her... Sue, proudly sitting, singing, and openly using sign language to the song being sung. There were no deaf people there. It was a very small room with no more than fifteen to twenty people celebrating mass. I was so relieved to know that she was there. I didn't care about anything else. I saw the look of shock on her face when she saw me. I guess she was wondering how I could have made it. I, too, was contemplating the same question as I eagerly awaited Communion, knowing that it was by the grace of God that I was there.

I was not angry. During the sign of peace, I walked over to her and hugged her. She said, "I'm so sorry." We went to our assignment after mass. I was so frazzled that I dropped a dish and couldn't concentrate. She asked me how I got there? I told her about my emergency money, but that I only had enough to get to the soup kitchen and not enough to get back home. She stated that she had the tokens, and she would give me enough to get home. I thanked her, and at that very moment, I realized that this was not my home.

After the weekend, Sister Rachel returned and immediately began digging into our weekend. Now she had material she could use to manipulate me against Sue...and she did. I was exhausted and now had taken my white ribbon off my keyring and carried it in my pocket.

From Shadows of Darkness to Silhouettes of Hope

I walked in on a conversation Sue and Sister Rachel were having, and Sister Rachel immediately began interrogating Sue. I was forced to watch. I closed my eyes, held my ribbon, and prayed. I couldn't take it. Over and over and over she questioned her.

Then, Sister Rachel pulled me in. She made me tell Sue how I felt. I told Sue, "You left me. You took my tokens. You wanted me to miss my assignment. You endangered my life. I have to know that the people I live with will protect each other. Why do you hate me?"

I was pushed over the edge. The lack of sleep had taken its toll on me. I was hungry. I was weak. I was right where Sister Rachel wanted me. When Sue answered my questions, I immediately knew it was due to manipulation. She stated she hated me because I was thin, and she was not. *What were they doing to her?* I cried. She cried. I hugged her.

I was so angry at the formation director for what they were doing to Sue. This was not the girl I knew a few months ago. The girl I knew was comfortable with herself. She would never have done the things she did over the weekend. No, she was changing, and it was due to this twisted form of manipulation that they called transformation. Sue was manipulated to the point of endangering another person's life.

The manipulation games were successful in driving us apart. Our only conversations were in public. We did have a brief moment to talk quietly in the kitchen one day. Sue was clearly distressed, as was I. We both agreed that we felt as if we were in a *Twilight Zone*. We both agreed that they were driving a wedge between us in order to keep us apart. We weren't sure what was happening to us, but knew it was not part of transformation. We both agreed that we wanted to get out. Sue also stated that Sister Rachel told her it was time to sell her van that she had arrived in. Sue had been under the impression she could keep it for the first year. She was concerned that her only means of transportation was being taken away from her. She didn't understand the reasoning behind selling her van. This was a year of discernment. Sue would need her van if she chose to leave. She was distressed and stated she had nowhere to go. Sue's fears included being left homeless and without a job. Her van would serve as transportation and possibly her home until she could get back on her feet. This was not transformation...It was nothing more than mind games of manipulation.

Sue had been led to believe that she had an eating disorder. She was not skinny but did not present with an eating disorder. She was now on a diet along with other sisters in the house. I felt this to be odd, as this was not really the time to be focusing on losing weight. Yes, eating healthy foods was important, as we had very active lives. To be placed on a diet at this time did not appear to be a healthy choice for Sue. I remembered Andrea talking about dieting and exercising while she was in the house last year also. I began to see a similarity within the different formation years.

I was losing weight rapidly because of the amount of walking and decreased calories provided for meals. My sleep was being affected due to the stressful situations I was encountering. I truly believed statements were being made and situations created in order to keep us awake and intentionally deprived of sleep.

While I was being deprived of sleep and food, I was clinging to God in prayer, begging for His help to endure this. I placed the ribbon back on the key, returning it to my end table. I wanted it to be the first thing I saw in the morning and the last thing I saw at night. By now, the ribbon, which was once bright, crisp and white, was now worn, tattered, and dirty.

I began to compare the ribbon to the way I was feeling. The ribbon was now taking on a different meaning to me. Night after night of prayer brought me to the words of God: "Whatever you do to one of these little one's, you do to me." My journey now took on a different light. My journey now had a profound depth.

CHAPTER 14

PUSHING THE BREAKING POINT

After two months of walking eight miles a day, I began to become weak. Breakfast consisted of toast or a bagel, a sandwich and piece of fruit for lunch, and a dinner prepared to accommodate those on a diet. I was losing weight fast due to the lack of calories taken in compared to the amount of calories used for my active daily routine. I knew I had to find a way to get more nutrients into my body. I thought about vitamins but wasn't sure they would provide enough energy. I thought about nutrition drinks and realized that would be a good solution. All I needed was a way to pay for them. I remembered having tried chocolate Boost, a supplemental drink, before. It was good. It was full of nutrients and was very filling. I now had to find a way to get some.

We took turns cooking dinner. When it was my turn, we had lots of carbohydrates. I remember cooking scalloped potatoes, pork chops, a hot vegetable, and bread. I was so hungry and couldn't wait to eat! I was scolded for all the carbohydrates I served, knowing that everyone was on a diet. I responded, "I'm hungry, and I'm not on a diet. I'm walking over eight miles a day and need carbohydrates. I've lost over twenty pounds in less than eight weeks!"

I was beginning to black out at times and would have to quickly sit down on my way to work in order to avoid passing out. I needed more food. I remember cleaning up the kitchen that night. I covered the leftovers only after stealing a bite of cold potatoes. They were so good. I swallowed the entire spoonful without chewing so I would not get caught. We were down to a maximum of one loaf of bread in the house at a time. The loaf had to be used sparingly. I asked for Boost to provide for my needed calories. I stated that I would buy it. I kept a credit card in case of emergency. I considered this an emergency. I truly felt I would die, and nobody would ever know the cause. The Boost was purchased using the household budget. I was asked what flavor I wanted. It really did not matter, but chocolate was my first choice.

By then, I trusted no one and was slipping into shock. I soon began to realize that matters of faith were being addressed, and I was being persuaded to alter my way of thinking to conform to theirs. I knew my faith. After all, I gave my life for my faith. I wasn't going to bend that which was so important to me. I gave my life to support and serve the Roman Catholic Church, not to fight it.

I was seriously concerned about Andrea at that point. I then totally understood her desperate phone calls from nearly a year ago. I was determined to see her.

Finally, a day was set aside for a visit with Andrea. Although it would be a few weeks away, I felt some relief. Sister Rachel had planned on driving Sue and myself to the house where Andrea was living. I no longer focused on anything other than our well-being, and preserving our faith. The road to holiness and transformation was no longer a priority. I wanted to see for myself that Andrea was safe and being taken care of. I didn't want to transform my ideas, my beliefs, and my foundation just to avoid the dark shadow that was slowly consuming my entire being. I didn't want to give in just to make this manipulation stop. I wanted to hang on. I wanted to keep fighting. I was in the midst of that spiritual battle...that Holy/Hell. I was not just observing it. I was actually living it!

Communication was an important part of this process. Every day was spent determining with whom I could have outside contact. They were immediately visited by Sister Rachel, who was now exerting her power over me with an abnormally authoritative force to include manipulation, isolation, and a newly added skill of interrogation.

I willingly gave all information that was requested. I offered the information about the lunch outing with the woman with whom I worked at church. Sister Rachel soon made an appearance at my job. The minute I saw her walk into the church office, I knew she was taking her manipulation game outside the house. What was once confined to the boundaries of the house was now entering into every aspect of my public life.

Sister Rachel entered the building and presented herself as a very caring, pleasant woman, speaking with everyone in the office. She politely excused herself, asking to remove me from work for a brief time to meet with her downstairs. She took me to the library, away from everyone. She quickly snapped; her personality changing in a split second. I knew at that time there was something terribly wrong. *Why couldn't this wait until I got to the house?*

She questioned something so unimportant that I honestly can't even remember what it was. It was just an excuse to enter my place of work. She then stated, with commanding force, that she knew everyone in the church office and would know every word I said to them. I stated, with assurance, "I don't speak to anyone about my life outside the house. I would never do that." I remained calm and assured her of my trust.

I was now afraid. No, I had not said anything to anyone outside the house. Instead, I had turned only to God. He was the only one I trusted. I had placed that keyring with the white ribbon tied around it on my nightstand every night. It was a reminder that God was with me. I was not alone. I spent the entire night, every night, in deep prayer. I would cling to God with all my might, my entire being, like never before. I would do nothing until I knew for sure what was taking place. I would do nothing until God showed me the way.

Was this part of transformation? Was this like the Marine training? Do they beat you down and then build you back up? My brother endured the training of the Marines, as did my son. Yes, they beat you down until you were exhausted and could take no more. Then, they built you up and turned you into a new person, a person with great confidence. They were totally fit. They were instruments ready for action and ready to protect our country with a bond so great that never would they leave one man behind. They were a team. No, by now, I was sure that was not a part of what was going on here.

I didn't understand why any of this was happening. I had not done anything or said anything that would initiate any of this behavior. I knew about obedience, followed all commands with love, and avoided all questions regarding their particular ways of carrying out a task. Pettiness was not a concern of mine at all. If a task was to be performed in a different manor than I would have done it, I did it the way they wanted it done. I would alter my way in order to conform to theirs. The task just wasn't important to me. I smiled and was thankful for the opportunity of humility. I went in prepared and was ready for these tests of humility.

What I wasn't prepared for was the lack of love and the manipulative ways of trying to succeed in changing my mind about significant things. I came to the realization that if there was no success in forming my opinion to align with their opinion about small, insignificant matters, I would most likely not be a successful candidate for this manipulation in large matters of faith. Finally, I saw the meaning of it all. The consequences became more severe when attached to matters of faith.

Timing was perfect. I was hungry, sleep-deprived, and exhausted. It was at that point that the matters of faith were targeted. The stage was set for the perfected art of brainwashing.

I had been exposed to some conversations with Sister Rachel, soon after I moved to the house. There were conversations regarding her opinions on varied topics of faith. It seemed she supported women becoming priests and had actually attended the ordination of a female priest. Of course, the Roman Catholic Church does not acknowledge these ordinations. A female priest is actually not even recognized as a practicing Catholic. I was happy to hear that this sister/priest was not from this particular order. I was upfront immediately with her regarding my disapproval.

Another conversation soon followed concerning Sister Rachel's opinion of reconciliation. She felt that she should be able to hear confessions instead of a priest. She stated that a person should not have to go through a traumatic experience one more time with a priest who lacks compassion when he/she has already poured out his/her heart to herself. Once again, I let my disapproval be known at the time.

Through my prayer, God was allowing me to see the truth. It took a very long time to discern what was from God and what was not. I felt it was more important to spend my nights clinging to my Lord in prayer, rather than sleeping. He would show me the way in my desperate hours.

I recalled my airline flight. That flight to holiness was truly a flight into the shadows of darkness. *What lay ahead in these shadows of darkness? Would I survive?* The next few weeks would send me plunging into a depth of darkness I never knew possible. It would test my faith to its limits.

CHAPTER 15

OUTSIDE INFLUENCE

Slowly, but surely, my outside influences were being cut off. I was neither allowed or able to talk to anyone at work.

Time was precious. My hair was taking too much time in the morning. I was spending so much time in prayer at night that I tried to get a couple of hours of sleep prior to 4:30 am. My hair had to go. I was given several salons to choose from. I was thankful for the opportunity to have the car by myself. I chose the salon closest to the house, to save time. As I slid out of the car, I heard my cell phone beep. I had accidentally pressed some buttons on the phone. I picked it up to clear what I had entered. I was taken by surprise when I saw the numbers 666, a scriptural reference to the mark of the devil, appeared on my phone. My stomach turned a flip, and I quickly cleared the numbers. I got back into my car and drove to the mall. I'm not necessarily superstitious, but under the circumstances, I wasn't taking any chances. After all, I had been praying for some kind of sign from God.

Upon returning to the house, I was greeted by Sister Rachel's approval of my haircut. She had also gotten hers cut recently. I felt a sigh of relief that there was not a confrontation of any kind at that time. I welcomed a brief moment of peace. Of course, it would not last for long, because as soon as I came back downstairs, the interrogation started. Where did you go? Who cut your hair? I was beginning to recognize the difference between casual conversations and interrogations. I calmly answered all of Sister Rachel's questions without hesitation. Then, she began her technique of intense interrogation. She insisted on knowing the person's name who cut my hair, stating that she thought she might go down the next morning to have a chat with her. I came back with an unexpected statement. "You just got your hair done last week, why would you want to go to her tomorrow?" I was not stupid enough to take the chance of having told this person who cut my hair anything about my situation. I knew this confrontation would be coming. Therefore, I got the stylist's business card just for that purpose. "I just happened to get a business card. I'll go upstairs and get it," I calmly stated. I removed myself from the table, retrieved the card, and gently placed it in front of her. "You will be pleased with her. She does good work, and she's very nice." I added information about her description and walked away. Sister Rachel was not going to intimidate me, although she was successful in cutting off all my avenues of communication.

Other people were being brought into the house to address faith "issues." By now, I was struggling physically as the lack of calories was still a problem. I was given a six-pack of chocolate Boost, but was drinking them sparingly. I did not know if I would be provided any more. At this point, I was doubtful. Using my credit card was not an option until I could leave. If I had trouble getting out, which I was suspecting, I would have no means of paying the balance on my card. That would create further problems down the road.

One evening, we provided dinner for a guest, who was to come for an evening retreat. It turned out to be another manipulative evening, this time on homosexuality. Everyone knows the church teaches that marriage is a sacrament between men and women. Everyone else is expected to live a life of celibacy. It is very simple. There is no room for homosexuality or even the discussion of it. One is to love and respect all people, without supporting the individual's sin. We are all on the road to holiness. We are all trying to overcome our individual sins. The sin of homosexuality is no different.

As the topic arose, I drifted away and recalled a dinner during which I volunteered Sue and myself to host. It was for the sisters located down south. It was held the night prior to our vote for acceptance into the Candidacy Program. Preparing the dinner was challenging, which I expected. We had prepared dinner for a handful of people, but the phone kept ringing with information that more and more were coming. These are normal challenges of formation that would prepare us for living in community. I thought it would be fun, knowing we would do just fine.

Sue began to get visibly upset and I reminded her that we were just being tested. I felt that we did fine, with the exception of one decision regarding a small bowl of meatless sauce we had set aside for the possibility of someone who didn't eat meat. We were barely going to make it with the amount of food we had as they were sitting down at the table, when one more unexpected person arrived. Together, we decided to combine the meatless sauce into the sauce with meat. We just did not have enough sauce for twelve people. I had previously made sure that there would not be any vegetarians for dinner. We felt as if we were making the right decision. We were corrected, and Sister Grace took out a frozen bowl of sauce from the freezer that she had made a few weeks ago. We quickly put it in the microwave to thaw. The lesson learned was that we had to be prepared hostesses. We had to think about the needs and wants of every guest at the table. If there happened to be someone there who did not eat meat, we had nothing for them to eat.

As we were eating, one of the sisters brought up the topic of homosexuality. As other sisters added comments, it was obvious that she had additional support. I prayed. I spoke with a calm, but confident voice. "The church teaches that homosexuality is wrong, but I truly feel it is possible to love the person without loving or supporting the sin." There was total silence. You could have heard a pin drop. It was an awkward moment, and I thought I should offer to pass around the bread, since I was hosting this dinner. I would not let their silence alter my opinion. I did not feel I owed an explanation either. It was simple. The church does not support homosexuality. They knew my stance on this topic. Since they accepted me into the program, I felt sure that this was not the overall opinion of the order itself. I felt it was just a few sisters voicing their opinions at that time.

As my mind drifted back to the current situation, I realized the topic of homosexuality was once again going to take place during dinner. I was thankful, because it gave me the opportunity to change the subject.

Dinner did not go well, as the meat was not cooked long enough. Several days before the dinner, Sister Rachel had stated that she wanted to cook a particular kind of roast and asked my opinion on the length of time to cook it. I had no idea, offering that maybe a couple of hours would be sufficient. It smelled great. Everyone was seated at the table waiting for it to be served. I already had determined what the topic of conversation was going to be, and therefore had already put up a barrier to Sister Rachel. I knew what was going to happen. A night of interrogation. A night of defending our faith.

Sister Rachel pulled the roast out of the oven and placed it on the counter to cut. It looked beautiful until it was cut. Red blood began to trickle onto the counter. The farther she cut, the larger the puddle. I couldn't help laughing. She cut as much off as possible, turning it from side to side in order to provide enough for the platter on the table. We placed the remaining roast back in the oven and, as we were wiping up the puddle of blood, our guest walked into the kitchen. I couldn't help laughing again, as Sister Rachel shielded him from the sight. Maybe it was the stress of knowing what the evening was going to turn into. Maybe it was the stress of all that had happened thus far. Maybe it was because I was actually seeing the irony between the roast and myself. I felt as if I were the roast, and someone was slowly cutting into the depths of my soul until blood poured from my side. Placing the roast back into the oven just represented me being thrown back into the fire until I could take no more. They wanted me to conform to their way of thinking. This was not going to happen. No, I would rather die. The guest represented God entering unexpectedly, catching Sister Rachel in the act. I knew God would eventually appear... saving the faith, saving souls.

Humor was my only way to survive. I had to find humor in the dark shadows that were consuming me. We survived dinner, and then we watched a movie together. I remember thinking what a welcomed surprise. Maybe this was not going to be a night of interrogation, and my heart was lightened.

How could I have been so stupid to think the evening was going to be that simple? The movie was one with great emotion about a homosexual young man. It would make anyone want to support him. Yes, I had compassion for this man. Yes, I felt his deep pain. Yes, I would love him and support him.

Then it started, the interrogation. It was turned around completely. They were doing a good job of convincing us to believe this young man deserved the same pleasures in love; that it was a gift from God. Love was presented as a God-given gift for all, and He would not want even one of His children to be deprived of this gift. After all, God made them this way. Oh yes, they were so good at what they did. I was so angry. I kept thinking about my previous priests and putting them in this situation. None of them would have ever shown a film like this. They would have never used it to condemn those who did not support homosexuality. Yes, homosexuals deserve rights, but this was not our faith. My anger became so deep as they tried to change the teaching of our faith. I was so angry, I removed myself from the room.

The conversations continued over the days ahead. There were conversations that included how God wanted everyone to be happy. He would not want a homosexual to be deprived of those pleasures offered to everyone else. Everyone needed and deserved intimacy. I stood by my beliefs. I explained my stance on the topic and did not feel the need to argue it. I wasn't going to change it.

The consequences of not agreeing with these opinions were becoming more severe. I was isolated and had no one with whom to talk. I finally realized I must go to the priest. I wanted out. I had made a reference that I would like to celebrate the Sacrament of Reconciliation. I had been attending mass alone up until that point. A couple of days later, Sister Rachel stated she wanted to attend morning mass with me. She insisted on driving me. There was silence, and I tried to make light conversation. Once Mass began, I realized immediately that she had spoken to the priest after my request to go to confession. The homily was about allowing oneself to be transformed and not to fight the process. The priest looked me straight in the eye as Sister Rachel sat by my side. I knew at that moment that my avenue of communication with the priest at that church was now cut off. If he only knew the truth. If he only knew that the formation he was talking about was one of brainwashing...to indoctrinate so thoroughly as to effect a radical change of beliefs.

We were in complete silence on the way home from church. I was forced to listen to a talk show on the topic of homosexuality. I do not know if it was actually coming from the radio or a compact disc. I quickly began a conversation in which Sister Rachel would not participate. She made me listen to the talk show. I did not respond. I looked out the window and prayed.

I was very relieved when we pulled into the driveway. The car stopped, and I quickly opened the door to get out. She shouted, "Shut that door!" I stated, "I have to get to work." She shouted again, "Get back in this car, and shut that door." I got back in. I closed the door. The doors locked. She stated that I wasn't going anywhere. She went on to talk about the house in which sisters who had emotional or eating problems were housed. I had heard of this house and knew it was a reality. They quickly put everyone into a category with emotional problems or eating disorders. This house was then used as a threat. If you didn't conform to their beliefs, you were sent to this home where you received the medications and treatments each individual needed.

She stated that the movie we had viewed would be viewed again. She thought I just needed a little more time to think about it.

At this point I was terrified of her and knew I had to leave. I knew I had to play the game until the right opportunity presented itself to ask permission to leave. I listened in silence, refusing to talk. Finally, I stated, "The people at the church will be looking for me if I'm late. They will know something is wrong. May I leave?" She unlocked the door, and I told her to have a good day.

Once again, I requested a spiritual director and was denied. I stated that I had so much to discern and really needed an outside voice. In desperation, I suggested that Sister Rachel come with me. I had nothing to hide and would love to have her accompany me. Finally, I found a way to possibly escape any more harm. The more she felt I depended on her, the less harsh the treatment was. I thought for sure, any spiritual director would notice something was wrong even without the use of words. I longed for the meeting, which was immediately scheduled. I finally felt this would provide an opportunity to leave. I felt surely Sister Rachel would be advised that I would not be a good candidate for their order. I was filled with anticipation and looking forward to the meeting.

The spiritual director they selected to talk with me was from a different denomination. I felt that was strange, but I did not care at that time. In fact, I felt it might even be better. A total outsider was what I needed...someone I could trust. I would speak the truth, and I knew anyone hearing this truth would immediately call the police, then I would be allowed a way out. We walked to an office, which was locked. It appeared the person with whom we were to meet was not even in her office. I became suspicious. *Did we even have an appointment? Was this all just an appearance?*

We went back to the car to wait for a while. As we waited, Sister Rachel told me that the person we were to meet was a good friend of hers. I became sick. I began to sweat. Manipulated one more time. Just a moment after she told me this, the woman arrived. I had no time to think. I was shaking inside and out.

I asked for a cup of water. I was still shaking as I drank it. I was so obviously nervous that the cup shook. I knew I could not trust either of them at that point. I gave no information. I couldn't wait to leave. *Was there any place I was safe? Was there any person I could trust? Was it even possible to leave?*

I would play the game until I found a time to ask for a short break to go home. My phone conversations were being monitored. All phones were in open locations. I had no privacy. I did have my cell phone with limited minutes. I only had enough minutes for emergency phone calls. I had no money to purchase more minutes. I was trapped with no way out. I began to show dependency on Sister Rachel. This was the only way to receive some relief from the manipulation. Finally, we went out to dinner one night, and I was able to order anything I wanted. It was so good, and I pretended everything was just fine. There was a person making balloon animals. She made a diamond ring for Sister Rachel, at her request. She in turn gave it to me, taking a picture of "happiness."

Soon after, we were holding an event at the house. There would be a lot of people, and maybe there would be an opportunity for outside contact. I had hoped for an opportunity to meet someone from the outside.

It was a night of personality tests, the Enneogram, which was used to manipulate our personalities. I felt that one or more of the men who had signed up for the class was obviously planted in the group. I used humor to deal with all the manipulation and actually had a good time as I tried to manipulate them right back. I believe he picked up on my awareness and actually backed off. The man who was obviously staged in my group offered me his business card at the end of the night, but I knew better than to contact him.

Finally, the weekend came to visit Andrea. I couldn't wait to see her. She was living in a house about an hour away, preparing for her second year of formation. When I saw her, I was shocked at her appearance. She didn't look or sound good. She smiled, but something was very wrong. She served us something to drink and took me upstairs to see her room. As she lifted her long skirt to climb the stairs, she exposed her bruise-covered legs. I gasped and asked what had happened! She calmly lowered her skirt without expression and stated, "Oh, I'm so clumsy. I trip on these stairs so often." I knew without a doubt she was not telling the truth. She had a gray appearance to her face. Something was terribly wrong. She stated she had a cold. I replied, in front of everyone, "You need to see a doctor!" The subject was changed, and I felt sick. I met other girls in this group. They seemed to be from more traditional orders, some clothed in habits. I felt better knowing there were nuns from traditional orders there.

Our visit was short, and when we returned, I voiced my concern to the sisters about Andrea's appearance. Sister Grace, the vocation director, had come up from the south. I voiced my concern about Andrea's health to her. She made a statement about my weight loss. I stated it was because of the amount of exercise and the lack of calories. I also included the fact that Boost had been purchased to supplement my meals. I did not want to say anything further, knowing that I would suffer the consequences as soon as Sister Grace left the house. I knew I was not going to stay there. I was just waiting for the opportunity to present itself to leave. I was also beginning to wonder if I could even trust Sister Grace at that point. My goal at that time was to just get out. Once I saw the condition of Andrea, I proceeded quickly with my plans.

After Sister Grace advised Andrea to see a doctor, we were informed that she had pneumonia. I knew it without a doctor's visit. The blue-gray skin was enough to give it away.

After my visit with Andrea, I received a phone call from her. She stated the other sisters were giving her a terrible time regarding our prayer practices. She stated that the other sisters said we were required to pray the Liturgy of the Hours. The

Liturgy of the Hours is a form of prayer throughout the day, which all religious orders pray. Active orders do not pray the entire prayer throughout the day, but they do pray together as much as they possibly can, usually at morning and evening prayers. Knowing my conversation was being overheard, I encouraged her to do whatever she believed in. I so wanted to talk to her in depth, but it just wasn't possible. My only hope for her was prayer.

    I was alone. All outside people were or would be cut off or monitored. I had nobody to confide in. My only goal now was to find an opportunity to get out.

PART IV

BREAKING AWAY

CHAPTER 16

THE DECISION

I had made the decision to leave and was just waiting for the opportunity to do so. I continued to show my dependency on Sister Rachel in order to provide an avenue of trust that might open a door.

Although I had a credit card for an airline ticket, I would still need cash for my trip home. I also needed confirmation. *Could I just be under stress?* I was so sleep-deprived that I was not trusting my own thoughts. I had given up so much for this life. If I stayed, the manipulation would continue until my beliefs were changed. I did not want to change my beliefs. It was obvious that they were not going to stop. *Would God truly want me to stay until I collapsed? What good would that do?* Nobody would ever even know the truth. Nothing would be accomplished. No, I was pretty sure God wanted me to move on.

The temperature was dropping very fast. My morning walk to mass was now in the dark of night, with light appearing only after the dismissal of mass. The cold walk was creating pain in my chest, and the rainy days were becoming a dreaded adventure. My shoes were not appropriate for such cold temperatures, and the ankle-deep flood waters kept my feet moist all day.

I welcomed a gift of boots that had been left behind by one of the other postulants. I felt my newly developed dependency on Sister Rachel was paying off in small ways. I was so thankful for those little gifts that made such a big difference in my daily life.

I stayed focused as I carried out my daily routine. I was oblivious to the possibility that anyone would even notice or question my routine. I entered the church one morning, collapsing on the stairs that led to the church office. I carried out my routine of removing my boots, replacing them with work shoes, and shedding the layers of clothing needed for the long walk. This one particular morning was a little more challenging with the harsh elements. I had battled gusting winds and cold rain that particular morning. My umbrella had suffered damage as a result of the most difficult walk thus far. I was happy as I offered it up as a sacrifice to God and was looking forward to entering the warm office. I could have asked for a ride from Sister Rachel, but I knew it would come with another interrogation.

Normally, I was able to go through my routine in the hallway without being noticed. This morning was different. One of the women in the office showed great sympathy and concern for my well-being. I assured her I was fine. These were the only people I had left for regular conversation. I loved walking up those stairs into an atmosphere of kindness and love.

I had toyed with the idea of talking to the Monseigneur, but fear prevented me. I was still unsure of the connection between the order and this church.

By afternoon of that same day, the sun came out, and I chose to eat my lunch on a bench outside the chapel. I loved watching the people coming in for prayer. As I was eating, a lady approached me. I had remembered her face from mass. She was a very pleasant woman and was interested in my life. As we sat on the bench, Monseigneur approached us with his dog. It was such a welcomed blessing. He stopped briefly and talked for a moment while I petted his dog. He politely excused himself and returned to work. I watched as Monseigneur and his dog walked back to the church.

From Shadows of Darkness to Silhouettes of Hope

This very pleasant conversation the woman and I had been having turned within a split second. That same woman looked around, grabbed my arm, and said, "Sit down." My insides turned flips. I knew what was coming...interrogation from a stranger. I felt my lunch come up to my throat. She looked me in the eye and queried, "How did you get involved with those people in that order?" I was full of fear. *Was this a setup?* I was silent. I did not know what was happening. *Had this woman been hired to check me out? Would my words get back to the house?* I spoke very slowly, "I was involved with the sisters down south. The formation house is here. They sent me here." I felt that was a safe answer, not knowing who had set this little meeting up. Never moving her eyes from mine, she spoke again, "Get out. Get out now, while you still can!" I could not breathe. I truly felt sick, trying to discern if this was set up by the order, or if it was my answer to prayers. Then there was confirmation as she made one last statement, "I will deny what I just told you until the day I die. Get out, and get out now!" She walked away without another word.

I sat on the bench, frozen...unable to move. This was it. This was the confirmation I needed. I was terrified and shaking like a leaf.

That same afternoon, I was approached by Sister Rachel with a piece of paper. It was a request for allowance for transportation to work. I signed it without questioning it. I accepted it with gratitude. I would soon be catching the bus that stopped in front of the house, and it would drop me off at the church door. It seemed I would not receive the allowance for a couple of weeks though. It had to go through the process of approval first.

Would I be able to hold on? Would the approval be based upon my willingness to conform to their way of thinking, or did the church have something to do with this? Had someone from the church called with concern for my well-being? Was this just a coincidence? My mind was racing. If the church had anything to do with this, I knew there would be consequences attached. Only time would tell.

The words of that mysterious woman replayed over and over every night. My room was cold and seemed to be getting colder each and every night. No matter how many blankets I piled on top of me, I couldn't stay warm. It was so cold that I had to speak up. I was offered a heated mattress pad by one of the sisters. I accepted it with gratitude, as I was able to get a little more rest. I found if I kept turning over, warming one side at a time, I could sleep for short periods of time. It was so cold one night that I even got up to see if I could see my breath as I breathed into the cold air. Much to my surprise, I could not. My bones actually hurt from the cold, and my muscles ached.

My concerns regarding the temperature were met with sympathy, and I was led to believe it was all in my head, as my room was the same temperature as the rest of the house. I never mentioned being cold again.

The days passed, and Halloween was just around the corner. The fall decorations of pumpkins, scarecrows, hay stacks, and ghosts added some variety to my cold walks. The afternoon walk home was the most beautiful. The sun was warm, and the air chilled as showers of leaves fell into the streets and covered the sidewalks.

Yes, there was just something different about the fall season in the northern part of the United States. The trees were bursting with colors of red, orange, and yellow. I would imagine the leaves to be graces from God falling from heaven, creating a colorful path to follow. I knew He would soon create a path for me to leave. I was just waiting for His timing.

Our next outing, which would test my liturgical knowledge, was to attend a mass held at one of the other convent houses across town. The house was very modern. I was intrigued with the unique chapel, as it was a very creative addition to the traditional house. The celebration of mass was a warm welcome, which I embraced until the priest sat down after the reading of the Gospel, allowing a sister to carry out the homily. It was a very lengthy homily. I remember not one word of it. My focus was on the Liturgical Rules of the Roman Catholic Church regarding the homily, which was to be presented only by an ordained minister. At least I had time to contemplate my actions while she was speaking. I knew I was waiting for a way out. Therefore, I decided I should not make any more waves.

After mass, everyone was congratulating the sister for her wonderful homily. They continued to use the word homily over and over again. One would have used the word "reflection" if they were trying to "get by" with bending the rules of the church. It was obvious that they were boldly stating the fact that women had the right to give homilies during mass. I was not surprised at this but was more surprised that the priest had allowed it.

Sister Rachel knew my previous role in liturgical preparation. She knew I would have disapproved of this. I was not going to play this game any longer. I was sure she would think about the statements I made and come to the realization that they had drifted away from our faith. I was wrong. I was very wrong. They could not see how they had drifted from the very foundation of our faith.

I had sat in the mass thinking about the words of the stranger, "Get out. Get out now, while you still can!" Yes, this time I had to take a different approach. I needed that transportation money. It was the only means I had of getting any cash. Therefore, I had appeared to be supportive after Mass, waiting in line, congratulating the sister on her wonderful homily. I knew this was my ticket out. I talked to everyone about how I had enjoyed the mass and how much I enjoyed the homily. I felt as if I were finally welcomed within the order. I also felt deep grief. I was betraying the faith I loved so much. I saw no other way out.

I sat in the backseat of the car on our way home. I pondered my possible ways of escape. I would never make it until Christmas, and I would definitely never pretend to conform to their ways for a full two months. That was just not an option. The guilt was consuming me already. My next option would be to speak to one of the priests at the church where I worked. It was my last resort. I would make the attempt the next day.

    I was still filled with joy...nothing could take it away. God would provide for me. I did what He asked, and He would not leave me here. He was present. In all this mess, He was with me, and I knew He would save me from this nightmare.

    I went to work knowing that my release was just around the corner. The priest would help me, and I would be on my way home soon. I felt it in my heart. I would soon be free. My plan was interrupted when all the priests were out of the office that morning. I would have to wait. Surely I could make it a couple of more days.

    I stayed away from everyone in the house as much as possible. I logged onto the computer to check my frequent flier miles to see if I had enough miles for a one-way ticket home. I kept the door open to see if anyone was approaching the computer room. My hands were shaking. The computer was so slow. Finally, the airline website popped up, and I had actually remembered my password. I gasped...I stared at the amount of miles earned from my last flight, which was the flight to the convent. The frequent flier miles earned were 666. Once again, the numbers 666 had appeared. I had flown quite a bit over the last few years and not once had a flight earned an odd amount of miles. The normal amount was 250, 350, or any even number of miles. I shut the website down. I pulled it up again, thinking it was my eyes playing tricks on me. No, there it was again. I was determined to leave as soon as possible. I was getting out and getting out fast.

    I did not sleep much that night. I had a dream. Satan stood before me, a sly, sneaky grayish metallic figure. He was so deceiving. He smiled, and through a whisper of laughter, floated around me stating, "I have you right where I want you. Yes, you have everything you need." The ominous laughter continued.

    The next morning was Halloween, and I was looking forward to work. I knew the children would be out trick-or-treating on my walk home. I had my usual cup of coffee and entered the chapel, where I started every day with prayer and quiet time. I took a deep breath, walking slowly toward the altar with my eyes closed, thanking God for another day. I exhaled, opening my eyes with a slight smile on my face, knowing He was with me.

As I opened my eyes, I saw the front of the altar and was shocked...I could not even speak! Staring back at me were evil clown faces that had been attached to the altar! I closed my eyes. I knew my eyes had to be playing tricks on me. I had not slept much the previous night and was afraid the lack of sleep was now physically affecting me. They were evil clown faces...the kind in a horror movie, not a cute clown.

I ran out, back to my room before anyone saw me. I closed the door behind me. I gasped. I held my head and pulled my hair. *Am I awake? Is this a dream? What is going on?* I had to compose myself. I had to go back to the chapel. I was thankful I went in early and nobody saw me, giving myself time to prepare for another entrance. I went for another cup of coffee, appearing to be running late. When I finally reentered the chapel, I was expressionless. I glanced at the clowns, opened my book, and said good morning.

Sue entered and began discussing the clowns with me. I brushed it off stating it must be for Halloween. I returned to my prayer book. Sue followed my response.

When Sister Rachel entered, it was quiet, and we were ready for prayer. She was the one who had placed the masks on the altar. Her prayer service was about masking our true personalities. She thought the day was appropriate for this topic. In my eyes, it showed a lack of reverence, and I couldn't get past that to even pray. I was beginning to notice that God was very seldom the topic of our prayer services. Our prayer services were more focused on us, which caused even more alarm.

I was slowly detaching myself from everything in the house. I was not responding to anything. I was very polite but very distant. I gave no information. I did not speak up regarding conflicts of faith or liturgy. I was not doing this any more. I was silently slipping into my own world in order to escape. I could no longer take anymore. My faith was being shredded right before my eyes. Everything I was, everything I stood for, was ridiculed and distorted.

Thinking that detachment would help matters, I inevitably instigated the manipulating games to an even deeper level; a level that seriously threatened my well-being. The manipulating tricks were now used to threaten the level of my sanity. I was at the point of collapsing, extremely weak, and could find no response that would benefit me. No matter how I responded to their bizarre statements, it could and would be used against me. I did everything I could possibly do to remain sane. I would sneak off to bed in order to avoid any confrontations. I had to escape it. I had to sleep. I was so tired.

One evening, just as I turned the corner and quietly climbed the stairs to escape to my bedroom, I heard Sister Rachel's office door open. A tear dropped on my cheek. I prayed, please...no more. And then, the dreaded words stung my ears, "Dorothy, I need to see you!" My knees dropped on the stairs. I did not have the strength to stand up. I clung to the rail crying. I couldn't allow her to see me like this. That was what she wanted. I used the last ounce of energy to pull myself up, just in time.

As she turned the corner, she had no sympathy. I cried out, "Please, no more. Please, stop. I have done nothing. I cannot do this any more!" I was crying uncontrollably, and yet she still had no compassion.

She forced me into the library. She yelled, "Sit down!" I was too exhausted to be mad. I did not understand what was happening. She was banging her hands on the table. "Who are you? Who sent you here? Why are you here?" I could not believe what I was hearing. Was this another part of the manipulation, interrogation, and brainwashing? I was so confused. I was crying so hard, I could not even talk. She kept yelling, "ANSWER ME!

From Shadows of Darkness to Silhouettes of Hope

ANSWER ME!" I was terrified of the look in her eyes. Nobody came to my rescue. Someone in the house had to have heard her tormenting me.

I felt I would die that very night. My body could not bear the weight of this any longer. The physical energy being used while I cried uncontrollably was too much. I had to rest. It had to stop. *What kind of an answer was she looking for?* I only knew the truth. In between sobs, I stated very quietly, "It started with the *Vision* magazine. I checked off three orders and requested information..." I told her the whole story about the boxes and sorting the information. My story ended with, "I was just following God, and this is where He led me." I said no more. I just cried. Her anger did not subside. She yelled, "Tell me the truth!" I didn't know what she wanted from me. I was too weak to talk any more. I whispered, "That is the truth." Disgusted, she finally sent me off to bed.

The next morning Sister Rachel acted like the previous night never took place. The transportation money had been approved, and next week I would be able to take the bus to work. The money was placed on my desk without notification to me. I found it accidentally, actually. Maybe she realized my condition was worse than she had expected. Maybe she, too, was afraid I wouldn't survive one more walk to work.

I rid myself of every ounce of fear. I was not staying one more night, and I would just tell them I was leaving. I would be honest. Sister Rachel did not see our faith as the gift that it is. It was that simple. I don't believe the way they do, and I do not want to conform to their way of thinking. I chose to leave. I asked Sister Rachel if I could see her that afternoon. I would just sit down with her later in the day and tell her the truth.

I went to work as usual, but the office manager knew something was terribly wrong. I told her I had to leave. She said the priests were out and asked if I had someone I could call. I did not want to worry my parents. I would call them after I had a ticket. I had a spiritual director from home, whom I could call. The office manager encouraged me to call him, allowing me to use a private office. The spiritual director was out of the office for lunch and would not be back until the next day. It was an emergency, therefore, the secretary gave me his cell phone number.

I called my spiritual director from my cell phone, on my walk home. It was a frantic call during which I stated several facts along with the information that I only had a few minutes of call time. I was clearly shaken. He stated that it did not sound like a healthy atmosphere, and I could just tell them I'm leaving. I stated that it was not that easy. My phone was beginning to beep as my minutes were almost out. I had enough time to say, "I am leaving, but if something happens to me, and I don't make it home...please have it investigated." It sounded so reasonable to me, but you must remember that I had been sleep-deprived for three months, had lost approximately thirty pounds, and had been fighting to remain sane through manipulative mind games.

CHAPTER 17

THE ESCAPE

I continued my walk home and was relieved to know that I was finally going to have a heart-to-heart talk with Sister Rachel. She was waiting for me when I entered. She invited me into her office as I wondered if this was actually the same woman who had interrogated me the night before.

I immediately began the conversation. I stated my desire to leave, and it was clear that it was not going to be an easy task. Sister Rachel was shocked that I even asked to leave. The manipulation began again; there was no way around it. She stated, "No, I need two more weeks. At the end of the two weeks, we can talk about it again." Her demeanor was changing, and my confidence that was present upon entering was now fading as I saw the woman changing back into the one with whom I dealt the night before. I wondered what she meant by the statement that she needed two more weeks. *What did she need two more weeks for? Did she think I would give in within two more weeks of this and conform to their beliefs? What did she mean?*

I tried another approach. I stated that I did not feel well. I could not stay. I needed a break. I said I would go home for a break and come back. There was no discussion. I was not leaving, and that was that. The turbulence building within her was evident, and I walked away, only after I had agreed that I would give it two more weeks.

I couldn't go through another night like last night. I was leaving, and I would do it without permission. *What would happen in two more weeks?* I wasn't going to stick around to find out. I believed with all my heart that my body could not endure two more weeks. Even with bus fare, I was not strong enough. I went upstairs to my bedroom, retrieved my billfold, and called the airline from the phone right outside my room. I had my credit card in hand. I was leaving, and I was leaving that night. No, I was not going to stay one more night in that house.

I pulled out my airline card and dialed the number. I was speaking to a very nice young lady who was searching for the next available flight. "There's a seat available on the last flight out tonight," she stated. Then, clunk...the phone was dead. We were disconnected. I hung up and tried again. The phone was still dead. A lay person was walking by, and I asked if she knew what was wrong with the phone. I was advised that Sister Rachel was working on the phone the previous day, along with the computer. I dialed again. This time, the phone rang. When the woman answered, I immediately gave her my credit card number first, in case we were disconnected. She stated she would charge the ticket, and I could pick it up at the airport. I thanked her so much and with relief, she began to reserve the seat. She sighed, stating, "I'm so sorry. The plane is booked now. The next flight doesn't go out until tomorrow morning. Let me see if we can book a seat on that flight..." Clunk. Once again, the phone was disconnected. I was terrified. I ran to the computer. I pulled up the airline, and while I was purchasing the ticket, the computer shut itself off. I could not believe what was happening. I was actually being prevented from leaving.

I ran to my bedroom, grabbed my transportation money, and stuffed it into my pockets. I ran downstairs. Sister Rachel was in her office with the door closed. I signed out of the house, stating I was running to the post office.

I did not have much time. I had several things to do. The first was to find a store within walking distance that sold airtime cards for my phone. I found a drugstore and charged the phone card to my credit card. To add the airtime on this phone, you had to call from a land line. I ran into a nearby office and asked if I could make a toll-free call from their phone. My hands were shaking, I was white as a ghost, and I was out of breath. I was trying to enter all the numbers to activate the card, but for some reason, the card would not activate. I tried again without success. I was shaking too much. I was too scared and unable to read the numbers and enter them into the phone. The receptionist was busy, and I thought I should leave and try to calm down. I thanked the lady for her help.

How would I be able to buy a ticket with no phone? Fear set in. *Did Sister Rachel really know I would leave without permission? Why would she try to stop me?* This is a discernment process. It hit me like a ton of bricks. I was actually being held against my will. I wanted to leave. *How could I?*

I walked past the Marine recruiting office. I saw a woman on the phone. Yes, that is what I would do. I would tell the Marines, and they would help me. I ran in and waited outside her office. The woman was on the phone for so long. There was no sign of her hanging up anytime soon. I did not have enough time to wait. I had to move on. As I walked, I rethought the Marine plan. I realized that it was probably not the best of plans. As I envisioned two marines, dressed in camouflage with rifles on their shoulders, I shook my head and laughed. *Would anyone ever believe this story?*

I saw an attorney's office next. I ran in. The woman looked at me with a face full of questions. I must have looked frantic. She asked if she could help me. I said, "Yes, you can. Are you by any chance Catholic?" She said, "Yes, I am." I was so thankful. I told her that I was trying to leave the convent down the street, and I needed to purchase an airline ticket. I told her that I had a credit card for the ticket, and the number was a toll free number. "Could I please just use your phone to purchase the ticket?" I asked her, knowing she would be understanding.

The woman excused herself and slipped into a small office. I overheard whispers for a few minutes, silence, and then more whispers. When she returned she stated "I am sorry. We cannot help you." I could not believe my ears. I stated again, in a whisper, "What? It won't cost you a thing. I have a credit card for the ticket, and it's a toll-free number." She repeated her answer, "I'm sorry, we can't help you." I walked away alone and, for the first time, I questioned if God was truly with me. *Had He deserted me?*

I knew I had to return to the house. Time had run out. As I walked, I began to think about the song *"Hotel California,"* where you can check out, but you can never leave. I was a prisoner, being held against my will. *Was this nightmare ever going to end?* I was leaving one way or another. I would not stay in that house one more night. I did not care what I had to do. If I had to walk to the airport, I would. I would find a way to escape.

As I approached Sister Rachel's office, I noticed the light was off, and she was gone. I asked a layperson where she was, and she stated that she had an urgent errand and would be right back. I flew upstairs. The phone was working! I added time to my cell phone. I ran down the hall, turned on the computer and purchased my ticket. The evening flight was already filled, and the only flight I could get was in the morning. I signed out of the house again.

I ran down the street and called my parents. "I'm coming home. Can you pick me up at the airport tomorrow morning? If anyone calls you, do not believe a word they say." My fear now was that they would do the same thing to my parents that they had done to Andrea's parents. I didn't care how crazy I sounded. I was leaving. I would soon be free!

It was all set. I ran home, tip-toed up the stairs, and called a cab. I told them I would be ready in one hour. I packed the most important things first. I would only be able to take what I could fit in my suitcases. I would have to just leave the rest. I didn't care about anything. I had my faith. Preserving my faith was the only thing of importance.

There I was, standing in the middle of my room with all the suitcases I could possibly carry. I would not be able to make two trips. I had to take with me only what I could carry down the stairs in one haul. I glanced at the pile and smiled. I knew I would probably drop one or two of the suitcases, but I didn't care. I would do the best I could to carry it all.

I had the most important items in a shoulder bag, which was secured around my neck. If this was the only bag I left with, I would be okay. Its contents included my important papers, family pictures, and a few important books. Right below the zippered case lay my Bible and Catechism of the Catholic Faith. Although I couldn't recall the scripture verse, I recalled the following words: "Enter a house and if you are welcomed, stay. If you are not, brush the dust off your scandals and move on." I wasn't actually sure if those were the correct words, but the meaning was there. I also recalled the words of the priest who stated during one of our retreats, "Get out of that house and don't go back." And the stranger's words, "Get out...get out now, while you still can." Yes, I had to listen to the voices around me. I had asked for a sign, and if I ignored these voices, I would face accountability for my actions, or lack thereof.

I looked around for the last time, asking for forgiveness for my previous state of despair while on the street. I knew God was with me. It was a weak moment, and I had been afraid. I picked up my keyring with the white ribbon and slid it into my pocket. I reached into my other pocket to feel the transportation money. I was free.

I took one last, deep breath, said a little prayer of thanks, and walked toward the bedroom door. I froze in my tracks as I heard a knock on my door. The blood felt as if it were draining from my head to my feet. I was terrified. I took a deep breath. There was the knock again. I couldn't move. I watched as the door slowly opened. A sigh of relief came over me as Sue appeared at the door. Her face seemed to change, and her eyes widened. She softly stated, "Everyone's in chapel waiting." I glanced at my watch. I had totally forgotten about the time. She continued to speak, "It's your turn for chapel." We looked at each other, and I smiled. She said "You're leaving? I'll just tell them you're not feeling well and try to stall them." I thanked her. I thought about inviting her to come, but she had to make that decision herself. I felt badly that I didn't include her, but I didn't know where she stood. We never had an opportunity to talk.

The timing was perfect. I would sneak out during chapel. I wouldn't have to wait outside too long. I didn't care. I would be free as soon as I stepped onto the sidewalk.

Sue didn't make it back to the chapel in time to stall them. Just as I was coming down the stairs, I was greeted by Sister Rachel. "Where do you think you're going?" I stated, "I'm leaving. I'm going home." She said I couldn't leave. I saw where this was heading and just continued to push my way to the door. I had to get out! She blocked me. "No, you said you would give it two more weeks!" Her anger began to build. I looked her in the eye and stated in a low, but firm voice, "I'm leaving. I'm leaving right now."

She began the interrogation as her anger built. She demanded I get in her car. I knew if I got in that car, that would be the end. I would either be driven to the "house" for treatments, or we would have an accident. I knew I would never make it home. I stated "No, thank you. I have already made arrangements."

Her demeanor changed once again. She became kind, as she saw I wasn't responding to her anger. I saw through her. I wasn't going to play these games any longer. She lacked something. She lacked love.

She insisted on driving me to the airport. She spoke in a kind voice, stating she felt responsible, and she wanted to do this for me. I responded simply with, "No, thank you."

Sister Rachel wouldn't allow me to get to the door until I told her what cab I had called. I felt it was over, and there was nothing she could do at this point, since they were already on their way. I gave her the name of the cab company and proceeded to the door.

I piled my suitcases on the sidewalk and began to sing "Amazing Grace." I felt it odd that Sister Rachel didn't follow me, and I began to wonder what she was up to.

As I was singing, I heard someone walking toward me. I stopped singing, frozen with fear. Then, I heard a familiar voice, it was Sue. She said the tires on her van had been either slashed or the air had been released. She thought Sister Rachel probably thought we were both leaving. She stated that she had to get back inside, but wanted to warn me of what she had done. We both looked at each other as I asked, "What is she capable of?" Sue answered "I don't know...I don't know, but I have to get back inside."

I waited for a cab that never came. It was now thirty minutes late. The number for the cab was upstairs. I could sneak upstairs while they were still in chapel to retrieve the number. I had to call. I had no way to leave.

I opened the door, leaving my belongings on the street. I quickly retrieved the number by the phone and ran back to my suitcases on the street. My biggest fear was that the cab office had already closed.

Finally, someone answered. They said they were on their way but got another call and had to pick up someone else. I immediately thought it was strange and didn't trust them. *Had Sister Rachel manipulated the cab company into picking up someone to follow me?*

I convinced myself that I was becoming paranoid and would be home soon. I continued to sing. Sister Rachel was in the driveway, by the backdoor. I figured she was just watching to make sure I was picked up safely. After all she was responsible for my well-being.

Finally, the van showed up. I was on the curb with my bags. All they had to do was pull up to the curb and pick me up. There was no traffic on the road whatsoever. The van didn't even slow down by the curb, but pulled right into the long driveway, stopping at the back door.

Now I was angry. I had called the cab specifically stating I was on the curb. I pulled my suitcases all the way to the van where Sister Rachel was and tossed them into the back. She once again asked me to stay. She was very polite, caring, and sincere. I thought it strange, and then I saw three men in the van, all within hearing distance. Her statements made me angry, for I knew it was all a facade. I knew without a shadow of a doubt that she was involved in the "delay," and the men in the van were most likely involved.

I got into the van and politely said hello to everyone. The driver asked where I was going...another red flag. I stated, "I specifically told dispatch that I was going to the airport." I began to feel fear up and down my spine. Was this actually a limo service? Did I just get into a van with people I don't know? He replied,"There are no more flights going out tonight. You don't want to go to the airport." I could feel the goosebumps forming on my arms, as I firmly stated, "Take me to the airport."

Fear consumed me. I had to let them know that someone knew my whereabouts. I called my brother, praying that he would answer the phone. "I'm out of the house. I'm going to the airport and will be home tomorrow morning." I felt better. If these men were involved in someway, at least they knew that someone else knew my whereabouts.

I remained silent until we got to the airport. I asked the driver how much I owed him, paid him, and retrieved my bags. He offered to help, but I refused, proclaiming that I was fine. I wanted to get away from them as soon as possible.

CHAPTER 18

THE FLIGHT HOME

There I was, on the curb of an airport that was closed. It was vacant. It was dark. It was in a bad section of town. It was going to be a long night. The door was open. I thanked God.

I sat down with my luggage, right inside the door. The wind was whipping in every time someone opened the door to enter. It appeared that the airport was a resting place for the homeless. The cold winter air chilled my bones every time the door opened. I just couldn't get warm.

It was obvious that I was waiting for a morning flight. I saw a man come to the counter from the back. I asked him if I could check my luggage in now for a flight for tomorrow. I didn't care when the bags arrived. I didn't even care if the bags got lost. I just didn't want to haul them around all night. I was very hungry. I wanted to see if there were some snack machines. He said he couldn't check them in until 6 a.m. There was nowhere I could store them for the night. I would have to carry them with me.

The man at the counter said it would be safer on the next floor and pointed to the elevator. He also reminded me of the two-suitcase limit and one carry-on. In all the excitement, I had forgotten all about that.

I piled my suitcases up and headed to the elevator. I honestly thought about stopping the elevator in the middle of the floor for safety, but figured an alarm would go off. I was hungry. My mission was to find some food. It was a small airport, not like those large ones that had fast food restaurants open twenty-four hours a day. I wasn't sure I would even be able to find food here. Oh, what I would have done for a hamburger!

I found a bench, making myself comfortable among the homeless. I guess it was a good place for them to sleep. It was not too warm, but it beat the elements on the streets.

I settled in and called my son, Chris. I told him I was safe, but I think he could hear the fear in my voice. My fear was that I would fall asleep and miss my flight. He was my support system throughout the night. We called each other off and on all night. I chose a bench close to the snack machines in order to keep from hauling my bags all over the place. I ate peanut butter crackers, chips, and coffee all night. I must have consumed a cup of coffee every hour. I was thankful that I had enough small bills, specifically for the bus fare. Between Chris and the caffeine, I was assured I wouldn't miss my flight.

I took a nap, bundled under my heavy coat. My cell phone was next to me so I wouldn't miss a call from Chris. He would be frantic if I didn't answer.

I woke up startled as someone yelled from the escalator, "Hey, wake up! Hey, wake up!" I jumped out of my skin in fear! I looked up and saw a man who appeared to be a janitor, waving his arms at me. He yelled over, "Put that cell phone in your pocket! Don't leave anything out in sight!" That was the end of my sleep. I was now too afraid to close my eyes.

I wandered around with my bags looking for a restroom. I knew I had to shed at least one suitcase. I chose to dump the one with the cloth strap containing all my important items. It was my favorite suitcase, but the least expensive to replace. I sorted through the items, cramming them into a larger suitcase, retaining those important belongings, and discarding items that weren't as valuable to me. I stuffed them in the trashcan, along with the suitcase. I was living a nightmare.

From Shadows of Darkness to Silhouettes of Hope

I looked into the mirror and didn't recognize the person I saw. I didn't even look the same. I was only gone for three months. My clothes hung off my bones. I was thankful it was winter. I could cover up with a coat and avoid any stares. I was so hungry. I needed real food. I felt for the homeless. I knew I was going home. I knew I would receive a meal soon. I couldn't imagine living like this every day. I couldn't imagine the endless hunger. I was so tired. I thought about my mother's meatballs. I could actually smell them.

As I pulled my suitcases back to my bench, I began to feel faint. I leaned against the cold window and drifted. I hid my purse under my coat and held my cell phone in my hand.

Once again, I was awakened by the janitor, who evidently watched my back all night. "Hey, wake up! Hey, wake-up! The front counter is open. Go check your bags. Don't miss your flight!" Yes, I believe in angels. I slept amongst the homeless in the airport, but there was an angel with us, watching over us throughout the night.

I checked my bags and found my terminal. Finally, I was on my way home. There were plenty of seats at the terminal. It was early, and I was on one of the first flights to leave the airport.

I stared at a man walking toward me, taking a seat in the chair right next to mine. I was tired. I pulled a book out and began to read, or pretended to read. This was not normal. People do not sit right next to a stranger when there are so many unoccupied seats available. I assured myself that I was just paranoid and tried to ignore the man.

The stranger wanted to talk...I didn't. I had just been through the worse possible nightmare I could ever imagine. Chatting with a stranger was just not appealing to me at that time. After all, I was hungry, tired, and actually becoming sick as the voices of people were drifting in and out.

He insisted on talking to me, which annoyed the hell out of me. He wanted to know where I came from, what I was doing, and where I was going. *What? Am I truly going crazy?* I thought to myself, this was not normal. I wanted him to go away. *More interrogation?* I thought I had escaped all of that. I didn't trust him. I actually didn't trust anyone at that point.

Recognizing my weakness, I gathered my thoughts. He introduced himself to me, and I politely introduced myself to him. The truth was not an option at this point. I responded politely, "I'm from Alabama. I work for the Department of Homeland Security. I'm headed home." He chatted briefly for a few minutes and excused himself. I noticed him at the terminal counter for a long time. I watched him walk away from the counter, and I never saw him again in the terminal.

I felt bad that I hadn't told the stranger the truth. I convinced myself it was a partial truth. I used to work for the Department of Homeland Security...or a company contracted by them. No, the truth wasn't an option. In fact, I didn't know if the truth would ever be an option.

It came time to board the plane. Finally, I had escaped. It was over. It was really over. We stood in a long line, waiting for our tickets to be checked. I still had an extra bag. Another person next to me told me that we were only allowed one carry-on, and I had two. I was too weak to respond. I couldn't hear.

Voices were drifting. I leaned against a wall and felt the blood wash from my face. My legs began to give out as I started to slide down the wall. I got hot.

I removed my coat, placed my shoulder bag over my shoulder, and put my coat back on. I wasn't going to throw away my purse too. My other carry-on was full of important things. Important papers, family pictures, etc. I wasn't parting with either of them.

The stranger said nothing more to me. It was obvious that something was terribly wrong. I'm sure people thought I was on drugs, had recently been released from prison, or was running from an abusive husband. I didn't care what anyone thought, but it was obvious that I had experienced something out of the norm.

From Shadows of Darkness to Silhouettes of Hope

The flight attendant took my ticket and said, "Have a great flight." I looked her straight in the eye. "Thank you" came out in a whisper. It was obvious that I had a very large bag under my coat and another in my hand. She turned her head. I was free.

I removed my coat as soon as I found my seat. I was thankful that my seat was in an exit aisle. I had plenty of leg room. I needed it for the extra bag. I was going to sleep the whole flight. I would wake up at my destination...HOME! I was so glad it was a straight flight. I didn't think I had the energy to make a connecting flight.

I closed my eyes as I sat in the center seat with an empty seat on either side. I had hoped that nobody would fill them. I wanted to be alone. I didn't want to talk. I began to drift immediately and was awakened by someone sitting next to me. She was a very nice, pleasant girl with headphones. Yes, I wouldn't have to talk, as she would be listening to music throughout the flight.

As I began to readjust my bags, making room for the woman, I caught a glimpse of a man walking down the aisle. I couldn't believe what I saw. It was the same man who had sat next to me at the terminal! I had an ominous feeling. There was something not quite right with this man. I wondered if he could possibly be following me. Once again, I told myself that I was just being paranoid.

I closed my eyes again and was quickly jolted into a panic attack as he called out his seat number about a foot in front of me. No. No. No. This could not be possible. This was not a coincidence.

He sat down beside me, and he continued to talk. I needed to sleep. I was afraid I would lose my temper with him if he wouldn't be quiet!

I did everything to keep calm. I even sang "Amazing Grace" quietly in my head. I tried to be polite. I didn't want to be rude. I had too many emotions spinning around in my head. I couldn't add a suspicious character who appeared to be following me to my paranoid behavior. Yes, I had convinced myself that I was paranoid and over-reacting to a man who obviously was just lonely.

Until...his statements had underlying meaning, and his interrogation once again began to show its face within a scenario that I could not escape! There was no escaping him. It was a long flight, and I couldn't get away from him. The more he talked, the more I knew that this was more than just a coincidence. When I realized that this was more than a coincidence, I told him firmly that I was tired and needed to rest.

It was at that point, he reached into his bag, and very slowly took out a can. He continued his movements in slow motion, reaching across my seat, floating the can in front of my face. He asked me to nudge the girl next to me. He spoke to the girl sitting beside me, "Excuse me, would you care for one?" Removing her earphones, she politely said, "No thanks," and smiled at him.

She returned her earphones to her head. He slowly moved the can in front of my face, coming to a complete stop in front of my eyes. It seemed as if time stood still; as if time itself had frozen for a few minutes. I couldn't breathe.

"Would you care for one?" he asked. My stomach turned, my heart beat uncontrollably, sweat poured from every pore in my body, and every hair on my head was standing straight up. I was not paranoid. I was not crazy. *Would this ever end?* I stared at the can, now floating in front of my face. I turned my eyes toward his, meeting for a brief moment. My face was expressionless as a slow, smirky smile appeared on his face.

Returning my eyes to the beverage, I couldn't bear the sight of it. I closed my eyes slowly relieving myself from the sight of the can still floating in front of my face. His face was now only a couple of inches from mine, and I could actually feel the warmth of his breath on my cheek. He asked again, "Would you care for one?" I opened my eyes and quietly answered, "No thanks, I can get one...at HOME." I watched the can slowly float away and back into his bag...the can of chocolate Boost.

CONCLUSION

THE MISSION

Fictional names and places have been used to protect the individuals in this true story.

Over the years, there has been a drastic decline of women entering religious life. There are many orders and many reasons for this decline. I just happened to stumble upon one of them.

People drift away from their faith. Nobody is immune from this. As Catholics, we are aware of this, and our participation in the season of Lent acknowledges our need to "Come back to the Gospel" each and every year. If we do not take that time to return to the Gospel, realigning our lives to be more Christ-like, we continue to drift farther and farther away. As I have said, no one is immune from this, not even religious groups.

There are many kinds of religious orders. Some orders are "papal" orders, who report only to the Pope. Others are local and report on a regular basis to the bishops. The order I was involved in was a papal order. The Catholic Church's hierarchy was established in order to preserve the faith. When a group of people has nobody to whom they can report on a regular basis, there is ample room for drifting away from the foundation of the faith.

What I have uncovered throughout this process is a great need for a vocation program for men and women seeking a life of service within a religious order representing the Roman Catholic Church.

The church supports and serves men seeking to be priests through the vocation department. The vocation director remains on the journey with the young men throughout the process. The church supports the men both emotionally and financially, allowing the vocation director to travel to their destinations on a regular basis.

The Catholic Church is also served by men and women seeking to serve as brothers or sisters, living in community with an established religious order. These men and women who seek to serve God by serving the Catholic Church with their entire life, deserve the same support and protection on their journey. The church has a responsibility to support and protect these men and women who enter religious orders representing the Catholic Church.

It is my mission to show the need for a vocation ministry within the Catholic Church designated specifically for religious orders.

It is also my mission to show the need for a discernment ministry established for all young people. This ministry would introduce them to all possibilities of vocations in life, whether it be single, married, or religious, beginning at a young age.

A portion of profits from this book will be donated for the establishment of this important mission.

May we seek to serve the Lord with love and support of each other. May God bless each person answering the call to serve Him, by serving His church. May God bless all those who recognize their course of drifting and return wholeheartedly to serve Him with love and compassion.

> May the peace of Christ be with you all,
> Dorothy Boozer